SCHOLASTIC

FAST START for Early Readers

by Nancy Padak, Ed.D. and Timothy Rasinski, Ph.D.

NEW YORK • TORONTO • LONDON • AUCKLAND • SYDNEY
MEXICO CITY • NEW DELHI • HONG KONG • BUENOS AIRES

Teaching Resources

For our parents and our children, who taught us the joy and value in parent-child reading activities.
—NP and TR

Acknowledgments

We have been working on *Fast Start* for about a decade, so it's impossible to list everyone we want to thank. From the very beginning, children, parents, and teachers have shown us ways to make the program more useful. We do want to offer special thanks to several people: Bruce Stevenson, a school psychologist in Worthington, Ohio, who demonstrated the effectiveness of *Fast Start* among children at risk for reading failure; Sharon Davis at Seiberling School in Akron; Mary Margaret Luchitz, the Reading Curriculum Specialist in Canton; and the Literacy Lead Teachers in Canton—all of whom enabled us to conduct research about the effects of *Fast Start*. We also thank Terry Cooper and Kama Einhorn at Scholastic, whose enthusiastic support and generous assistance allowed the project to come to fruition.

We gratefully acknowledge permission to reprint the following poems:

"Apples Three"© by Monica Kulling, from *Month-by-Month Poetry: September, October & November* (Scholastic, 1999). Reprinted by permission of Marian Reiner.
"Away We Go"© by Eleanor Dennis, previously published in *Poetry Place Anthology* (Scholastic, 1999).
"Baby Chick" by Aileen Fisher, from *Runny Days, Sunny Days*. Copyright © 1958, 1986. Reprinted by permission of Marian Reiner.
"Bake a Cake" by Teddy Slater, previously published in *Word Family Sing-Along Flip Chart* (Scholastic, 2003).
"Best Deal in Town"© by Betsy Franco, previously published in *Thematic Poetry: Neighborhoods and Communities* (Scholastic, 2002).
"Bill and Jill" by Teddy Slater, previously published in *Word Family Sing-Along Flip Chart* (Scholastic, 2003).
"Circle of We" by Teddy Slater, previously published in *Word Family Sing-Along Flip Chart* (Scholastic, 2003).
"City Music"© by Tony Mitton, previously published in *Thematic Poetry: Neighborhoods and Communities* (Scholastic, 2002).
"Conversation"© by Althea M. Bonner, previously published in *Poetry Place Anthology* (Scholastic, 1999).
"Days of the Week"© by Meish Goldish, previously published in *50 Thematic Songs* (Scholastic, 2001).
"Drip Drop" by Teddy Slater, previously published in *Word Family Sing-Along Flip Chart* (Scholastic, 2003).
"Fingerplay"© by Helen H. Moore, previously published in *A Poem a Day* (Scholastic, 1999).
"First Book"© by Linda Kulp, previously published in *Month-by-Month Poetry: September, October, & November* (Scholastic, 1999). Reprinted by permission of Marian Reiner.
"Flu"© by Terry Cooper, previously published in *Month-by-Month Poetry: December, January, & February* (Scholastic, 1999).
"Good-by and Hello"© by Barbara Anthony, previously published in *Poetry Place Anthology* (Scholastic, 1999).
"I'm Me!"© by Meish Goldish, previously published in *Thematic Poems, Songs, and Fingerplays* (Scholastic, 1999).
"I Talk"© by Magdalen Eichert, previously published in *Poetry Place Anthology* (Scholastic, 1999).
"Jump or Jiggle"© by Evelyn Beyer, previously published in *Poetry Place Anthology* (Scholastic, 1999).
"The Lesson"© by Jane W. Krows, previously published in *Month-by-Month Poetry: March, April, May, & June* (Scholastic, 1999).
"Listen!"© by Jacqueline Sweeney, previously published in *Month-by-Month Poetry: March, April, May, & June* (Scholastic, 1999). Reprinted by permission of Marian Reiner.
"May on the Bay" by Teddy Slater, previously published in *Word Family Sing-Along Flip Chart* (Scholastic, 2003).
"Maytime Magic"© by Mabel Watts, previously published in *Poem of the Week* (Scholastic, 2000).
"My Dog"© by Helen Lorraine, previously published in *Poetry Place Anthology*, (Scholastic, 1999).
"My Neighborhood"© by Betsy Franco, previously published in *Thematic Poetry: Neighborhoods and Communities* (Scholastic, 2000). Reprinted by permission of the author.
"My New Red Bike" by Teddy Slater, previously published in *Word Family Sing-Along Flip Chart* (Scholastic, 2003).
"My Nose"© by Dorothy Aldis, previously published in *Month-by-Month Poetry: December, January, & February* (Scholastic, 1999). Reprinted by permission of Marian Reiner.
"Oh, What a Shame!" by Linda B. Ross. Previously published in *70 Wonderful Word Family Poems* (Scholastic, 2003).
"One Magical Midnight" by Teddy Slater, previously published in *Word Family Sing-Along Flip Chart* (Scholastic, 2003).
"Opposites"© by Meish Goldish, previously published in *50 Learning Songs* (Scholastic, 1999).
"Rub-a-Dub Cubs" by Teddy Slater, previously published in *Word Family Sing-Along Flip Chart* (Scholastic, 2003).
"The Shape of Things"© by Meish Goldish, previously published in *Thematic Poems, Songs, and Fingerplays* (Scholastic, 1999).
"Sheep in a Jeep" by Teddy Slater, previously published in *Word Family Sing-Along Flip Chart* (Scholastic, 2003).
"That Marching Beat" by Teddy Slater, previously published in *Word Family Sing-Along Flip Chart* (Scholastic, 2003).
"Traveling, Traveling"© by Meish Goldish, previously published in *Thematic Poems, Songs, and Fingerplays* (Scholastic, 1999).
"Wait for Me"© by Sarah Wilson, reprinted by permission of Sarah Wilson. Previously published in *Thematic Poetry: Whatever the Weather* (Scholastic, 2001).
"Watering a Rose" by Teddy Slater, previously published in *Word Family Sing-Along Flip Chart* (Scholastic, 2003).
"Winter Night"© by Claude Weiner, previously published in *Poetry Place Anthology* (Scholastic, 1999).
"Winter Snow" by Linda B. Ross, previously published in *70 Wonderful Word Family Poems* (Scholastic, 2003).
"What Do You Need" by Helen O'Reilly, previously published in *70 Wonderful Word Family Poems* (Scholastic, 2003).

Every effort has been made to trace the ownership of all copyrighted material and to secure the necessary permissions to reprint these selections. In the event of a question arising as to the use of any material, the editor and publisher, while expressing regret for any inadvertent error, will be happy to make the necessary correction in future printings.

Scholastic Inc. grants teachers permission to photocopy the reproducible pages from this book for classroom and home use. No other part of this publication may be reproduced in whole or in part, or stored in a retrieval system, or transmitted in any form or by any means, electronic, mechanical, photocopying, recording, or otherwise, without written permission of the publisher. For information regarding permission, write to Scholastic Inc., 557 Broadway, New York, NY 10012.

Cover design by Maria Lilja
Interior design by Gerard Fuchs & Sydney Wright
Interior illustration by Maxie Chambliss

ISBN: 0-439-62576-9

Copyright © 2005 by Nancy Padak and Timothy Rasinski

Published by Scholastic Inc.

All rights reserved.

Printed in the U.S.A.

5 6 7 8 9 10 40 13 12 11 10 09

Contents

Poems & Family Pages

Welcome to *Fast Start*!

Learning to read is one of the most important accomplishments of early childhood. Success in reading leads to success in other areas of school and throughout life. Recent research has indicated that family involvement in children's literacy learning can have a dramatic impact on their reading success (Postlethwaite & Ross, 1992). Yet there are few proven and systematic programs for helping teachers involve families in their children's reading. That's why we developed *Fast Start*, a simple, engaging way for teachers to involve families in their children's initial steps toward becoming literate. It's an at-home, parent-child reading routine for grades K–2, designed to improve childrens' early literacy, word recognition, comprehension, and fluency abilities. Getting families involved in *Fast Start* goes a long way toward helping your whole class become successful readers!

Fluent reading can be described as "accurate," "quick," "with expression," "with good phrasing," and "in a meaningful way." Why is fluency so important? The analogy of fluent speaking can help us understand the importance of fluent reading. Fluent speakers actually help their listeners make sense of words and ideas by speaking quickly, using meaningful phrases, and embedding expression and pauses into their speech. In the same way, a fluent reader efficiently processes surface-level text information to make it as easy as possible to comprehend. Fluency, then, is the scaffolding that provides a supportive framework for lifelong learning.

Fluent readers are better able to identify unknown words and comprehend text. Moreover, children enjoy being successful in reading, and that helps them develop positive attitudes toward reading and about themselves as readers. Activity that is focused, intensive, engaging, and authentic will give many children a "Fast Start" in reading, and that's what this program is all about.

Enjoy!

Nancy Padak, Ed.D. & Timothy Rasinski, Ph.D.

Research Based, Research-Proven

Fast Start is based on fundamental principles of effective fluency instruction (Rasinski & Hoffman, 2003). Why is fluency the emphasis? A National Assessment of Educational Progress study (NAEP; Pinnell, et al., 1995) showed that nearly half of all elementary readers do not read with acceptable fluency. Moreover, fluency is strongly associated with comprehension and general reading achievement. Our own research also points to fluency problems for many elementary-grade children (Rasinski & Padak, 1998).

Recent reviews of research on reading fluency (Kuhn & Stahl, 2000; National Reading Panel, 2000; Rasinski & Hoffman, 2003) have determined that fluency is an important and necessary component of successful reading instruction. The research also indicates that reading fluency can be effectively taught.

In an early study of this method, Jay Samuels (1979) found that the benefits of repeated readings transferred to texts that children hadn't previously read. Other studies (Dowhower, 1987, 1994; Herman, 1985; Kuhn & Stahl, 2000) have validated the finding that repeated readings can help improve children's fluency, word recognition, and comprehension.

Fast Start takes fluency instruction into the home, using authentic texts and engaging activities. Several years of research have shown that reading growth among children who participate in *Fast Start* is significantly higher than growth among their peers who do not participate in *Fast Start*.

Fast Start in Action

The *Fast Start* routine is simple: for ten minutes each weeknight, families and children read a short poem and then engage in developmentally appropriate, skill-building activities together.

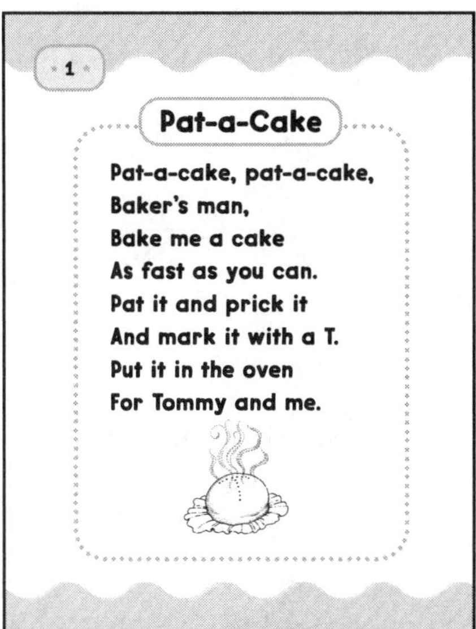

1

Pat-a-Cake

Pat-a-cake, pat-a-cake,
Baker's man,
Bake me a cake
As fast as you can.
Pat it and prick it
And mark it with a T.
Put it in the oven
For Tommy and me.

The Poem Pages

The sixty poems in the program have been selected for early readers. You'll find many classic nursery rhymes, simple, engaging poems, and even poems that can be sung to familiar tunes. There are enough poems to copy and send home one or even two per week for the better part of the school year. A few weeks into the school year, have families and children begin the program by spending at least two days with one poem. (For a more advanced class, you might send home four poems each week and have families work with a different poem each night. With this arrangement, you will complete the program in half a school year.) You can select poems according to curriculum themes or phonic elements (see pages 18–19), or simply go in order.

The parent-child reading has several purposes. Families model fluent and effective reading and provide support for children's efforts. The repeated reading leads to children's own reading fluency and sight word acquisition, and provides authentic texts for the development of additional reading skills and strategies.

The Family Pages

After parent and child have read the poem several times, they begin playing with the words from the poems. All these activities are quick and fun, and are designed for children to complete them successfully.

There are three levels of family activities based on the needs of the child. **Simply check the box next to the appropriate level on the log sheet (page 17).** In this way, you can use the same poems with all children, but differentiate the support children receive according to their developmental needs.

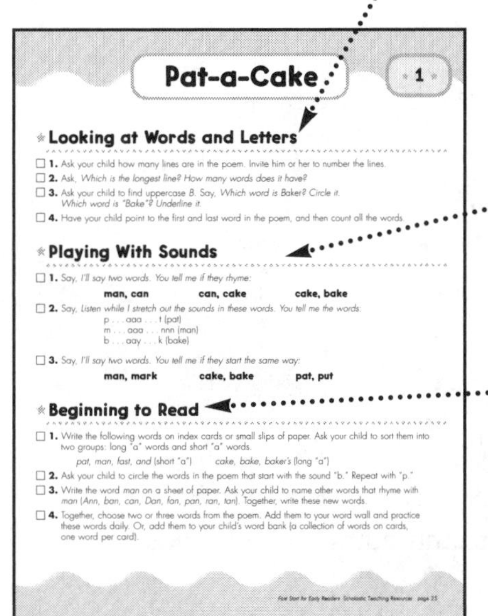

Pat-a-Cake

1

Looking at Words and Letters

☐ **1.** Ask your child how many lines are in the poem. Invite him or her to number the lines.

☐ **2.** Ask, *Which is the longest line? How many words does it have?*

☐ **3.** Ask your child to find uppercase B. Say, *Which word is Baker? Circle it. Which word is "Bake"? Underline it.*

☐ **4.** Have your child point to the first and last word in the poem, and then count all the words.

Playing With Sounds

☐ **1.** Say, *I'll say two words. You tell me if they rhyme:*

man, can **can, cake** **cake, bake**

☐ **2.** Say, *Listen while I stretch out the sounds in these words. You tell me the words:*

p . . . aaa . . . t (pat)
m . . . aaa . . . nnn (man)
b . . . aay . . . k (bake)

☐ **3.** Say, *I'll say two words. You tell me if they start the same way:*

man, mark **cake, bake** **pat, put**

Beginning to Read

☐ **1.** Write the following words on index cards or small slips of paper. Ask your child to sort them into two groups: long "a" words and short "a" words.

pat, man, fast, and (short "a") *cake, bake, baker's* (long "a")

☐ **2.** Ask your child to circle the words in the poem that start with the sound "b." Repeat with "p."

☐ **3.** Write the word *man* on a sheet of paper. Ask your child to name other words that rhyme with *man* (*Ann, ban, can, Dan, fan, pan, ran, tan*). Together, write these new words.

☐ **4.** Together, choose two or three words from the poem. Add them to your word wall and practice these words daily. Or, add them to your child's word bank (a collection of words on cards, one word per card).

Looking at Words and Letters
These activities, most appropriate for children who are just learning about reading, focus on concepts about print and letter recognition.

Playing With Sounds
These activities, for emergent readers, focus on phonemic awareness and word families, and are most appropriate for children who are just developing phonemic awareness and phonics skills.

Beginning to Read
These activities are the most developmentally challenging and focus on decoding words and sight vocabulary. They are designed for children who have begun formal reading and phonics instruction in school.

Introducing *Fast Start* to Families

Fast Start is a simple routine, but a formal and clear introduction for families is important. Families' role in children's literacy development is crucial. Observing a demonstration of the routine and having the opportunity to ask questions also builds families' confidence and promotes participation.

Early in the school year, offer two family "Introduction to *Fast Start*" sessions. Schedule these at convenient times, such as one in the early evening and another during the day. Or, use fall open house or back-to-school night to talk about *Fast Start*. Sustained participation in the program is much higher among families who have attended introductory sessions.

Before the introductory session, make copies of the following pages for each family. This is all they need to get started with *Fast Start*!

You can do the *Fast Start* orientation in four easy steps:

FIRST, introduce the program by stressing three points:

- This is an easy-to-do, research-based program that has been proven to make a significant difference in children's reading.
- It takes only ten minutes each weeknight.
- The routine has two parts: reading the poems, and doing the activities together.

page 9

Queridos familiares:

¡Bienvenidos al nuevo curso escolar! Aprender a leer será uno de los objetivos fundamentales de su hijo(a) este año. Cada día del curso, en nuestra clase nos esforzaremos por conseguirlo. ¡Y ustedes también jugarán un papel esencial desde la casa! Este año participaremos en el programa **Inicio rápido**. Este programa consiste en una serie de poemas cortos y actividades de juegos de palabras para que ustedes y su hijo(a) las realicen juntos. Por favor, dediquen 10 minutos cada noche a trabajar con su hijo(a) en este programa. A continuación, veremos cómo funciona el programa.

Cada lunes, les enviaré dos poemas, páginas para la familia y una hoja de lecturas en la carpeta de **Inicio rápido** de su hijo(a).

El método de **Inicio rápido** es sencillo:

Primero, lean el poema.

Después...

page 8

Dear Families,

Welcome to the new school year! Learning to read will be an important goal for your child this year. We will be working on this goal every day in our classroom, and you also have an essential part to play at home! This year we will participate in the **Fast Start** program. **Fast Start** is a set of short poems and wordplay activities for you and your child to do together. Please spend ten minutes on **Fast Start** with your child each evening. Here is how the program works.

Each Monday, I will send two poems, two family pages, and a log sheet home with your child in his or her **Fast Start** folder.

The **Fast Start** routine is simple:

Enjoy the poem together.

Then . . .

Spend a few minutes doing the activities on the family page. I will mark the log sheet to tell you which ones to use with your child, but feel free to try activities from the other two sections as well.

On the log sheet, record the amount of time you and your child have spent on the routine.

Please have your child bring his or her folder, with log sheet, to school each Monday.

And enjoy! As always, please contact me if you have questions or want to share information about your child. Together we will help children become strong and successful readers!

Sincerely,

page 10

1, 2, 3, Read!

The *Fast Start* Routine

Fast Start combines several principles of effective reading instruction. The routine is simple:

Read to your child,
Read with your child,
Listen to your child read!

1. **Read to your child.** Sit together in a comfortable, quiet, well-lit place. Read the poem aloud to your child several times, pointing to the words as you read. You are modeling fluent reading! Learning something is difficult if we don't understand what it should look or sound like. That's why reading aloud to children is so important.
2. **Read with your child.** Read the poem aloud several times with your child. Choral reading (reading aloud together with your child) is a very supportive way to introduce a new text. Don't be concerned if your child misses a word or two.
3. **Listen to your child read.** In this step, your child reads the poem several times to you! Offer lavish praise (and help, if necessary). Like musicians or athletes, readers must practice to achieve fluency. If your child stumbles on a word when reading independently, wait a second or two and then simply say the word. As your child's fluency increases, you might even tape-record him or her!

Then do an activity or two from the family page.
Keep the atmosphere gamelike and relaxed, so that children stay engaged and enjoy the interactions. You can check off activities as you do them. You might repeat the same activity until your child seems very confident doing it.

Follow this routine at least two days in a row for each poem.
Record your time on the log sheet after each session, to share information with the teacher and to help you keep track of your sessions.

page 10 Fast Start for Early Readers Scholastic Teaching Resources

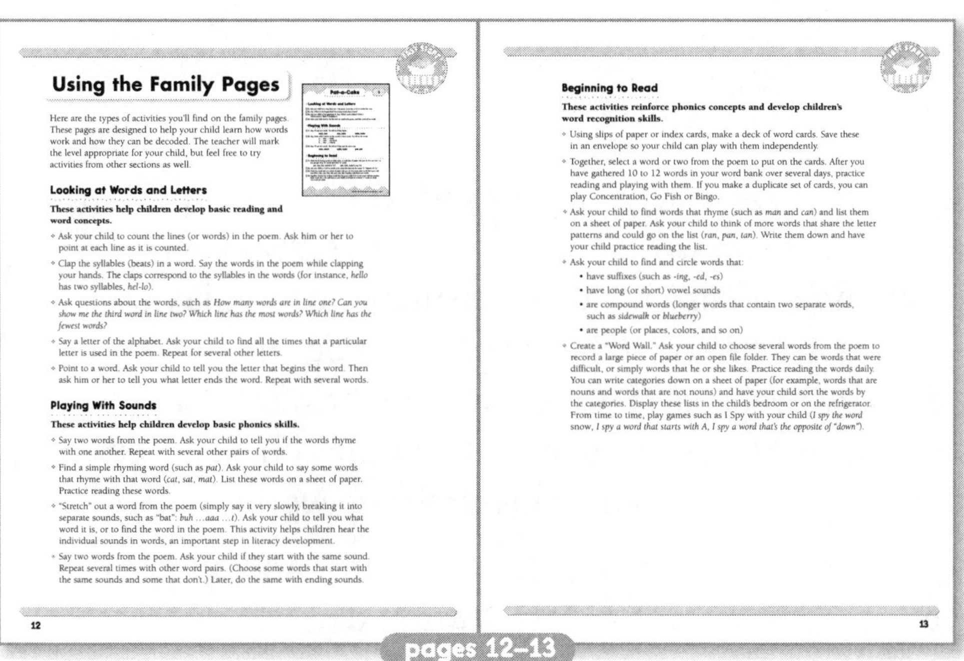

Using the Family Pages

Here are the types of activities you'll find on the family pages. These pages are designed to help your child learn how words work and how they can be decoded. The teacher will mark the level appropriate for your child, but feel free to try activities from other sections as well.

Looking at Words and Letters

These activities help children develop basic reading and word concepts.

- Ask your child to count the lines (or words) in the poem. Ask him or her to point at each line as it is counted.
- Clap the syllables (beats) in a word. Say the words in the poem while clapping your hands. The claps correspond to the syllables in the words (for instance, *hello* has two syllables, *hel-lo*).
- Ask questions about the words, such as *How many words are in line one? Can you show me the third word in line two? Which line has the most words? Which line has the fewest words?*
- Say a letter of the alphabet. Ask your child to find all the times that a particular letter is used in the poem. Repeat for several other letters.
- Point to a word. Ask your child to tell you the letter that begins the word. Then ask him or her to tell you what letter ends the word. Repeat with several words.

Playing With Sounds

These activities help children develop basic phonics skills.

- Say two words from the poem. Ask your child to tell you if the words rhyme with one another. Repeat with several other pairs of words.
- Find a simple rhyming word (such as *pat*). Ask your child to say some words that rhyme with that word (*cat, sat, mat*). List these words on a sheet of paper. Practice reading these words.
- "Stretch" out a word from the poem (simply say it very slowly, breaking it into separate sounds, such as "bat": *buh …aaa …t*). Ask your child to tell you what word it is, or to find the word in the poem. This activity helps children hear the individual sounds in words, an important step in literacy development.
- Say two words from the poem. Ask your child if they start with the same sound. Repeat several times with other word pairs. (Choose some words that start with the same sounds and some that don't.) Later, do the same with ending sounds.

12

Beginning to Read

These activities reinforce phonics concepts and develop children's word recognition skills.

- Using slips of paper or index cards, make a deck of word cards. Save these in an envelope so your child can play with them independently.
- Together, select a word or two from the poem to put on the cards. After you have gathered 10 to 12 words in your word bank over several days, practice reading and playing with them. If you make a duplicate set of cards, you can play Concentration, Go Fish or Bingo.
- Ask your child to find words that rhyme (such as *man* and *can*) and list them on a sheet of paper. Ask your child to think of more words that share the letter patterns and could go on the list (*ran, pan, tan*). Write them down and have your child practice reading the list.
- Ask your child to find and circle words that:
  - have suffixes (such as *-ing, -ed, -es*)
  - have long (or short) vowel sounds
  - are compound words (longer words that contain two separate words, such as *sidewalk* or *blueberry*)
  - are people (or places, colors, and so on)
- Create a "Word Wall." Ask your child to choose several words from the poem to record a large piece of paper or an open file folder. They can be words that were difficult, or simply words that he or she likes. Practice reading the words daily. You can write categories down on a sheet of paper (for example, words that are nouns and words that are not nouns) and have your child sort the words by the categories. Display these lists in the child's bedroom or on the refrigerator. From time to time, play games such as I Spy with your child (*I spy the word* snow, *I spy a word that starts with A, I spy a word that's the opposite of "down"*).

13

pages 12–13

Fast Start Log

For ______________________ Week of ______________

Please work on the activities in the section labeled:

☐ Looking at Words and Letters ☐ Playing With Sounds ☐ Beginning to Read

Day	Poem	Time	Comments
Monday			
Tuesday			
Wednesday			
Thursday			
Friday			
Saturday			
Sunday			

Fast Start for Early Readers Scholastic Teaching Resources page 17

page 17

NEXT, distribute colorful folders with pockets (one per family) and have parents put their papers (copies of pages 8–9, 10, 12–13 and 17) in the folders. Invite families to decorate their folder at home with their child. Put a *Fast Start* sticker (bound into this book) on each so children can write their names on their folders.

THEN, do a simple demonstration so families can see *Fast Start* in action. Refer families to pages 10 and 12–13 ("1, 2, 3, Read" and "Using the Family Pages"), and the poem (and corresponding family page) with which you have chosen to launch the program. Tell them that this will be the first poem in the program that they will enjoy with their child! Using a volunteer (another school employee, if possible) to play the child's role, demonstrate the entire guided reading routine (**read to** your child, **read with** your child, **listen to** your child read). Then, demonstrate several of the activities on the family pages (especially clapping syllables and stretching words, since these may be new to families). Point out the log sheet (page 17).

LAST, provide time for questions, and encourage families to contact you if they have difficulty sustaining the routine.

Dear Families,

Welcome to the new school year! Learning to read will be an important goal for your child this year. We will be working on this goal every day in our classroom, and you also have an essential part to play at home! This year we will participate in the **Fast Start** program. **Fast Start** is a set of short poems and wordplay activities for you and your child to do together. Please spend ten minutes on **Fast Start** with your child each evening. Here is how the program works.

Each Monday, I will send two poems, two family pages, and a log sheet home with your child in his or her **Fast Start** folder.

The **Fast Start** routine is simple:

Enjoy the poem together.

Then . . .

Spend a few minutes doing the activities on the family page. I will mark the log sheet to tell you which ones to use with your child, but feel free to try activities from the other two sections as well.

On the log sheet, record the amount of time you and your child have spent on the routine.

Please have your child bring his or her folder, with log sheet, to school each Monday.

And enjoy! As always, please contact me if you have questions or want to share information about your child. Together we will help children become strong and successful readers!

Sincerely,

Queridos familiares:

¡Bienvenidos al nuevo curso escolar! Aprender a leer será uno de los objetivos fundamentales de su hijo(a) este año. Cada día del curso, en nuestra clase nos esforzaremos por conseguirlo. ¡Y ustedes también jugarán un papel esencial desde la casa! Este año participaremos en el programa **Inicio rápido**. Este programa consiste en una serie de poemas cortos y actividades de juegos de palabras para que ustedes y su hijo(a) las realicen juntos. Por favor, dediquen 10 minutos cada noche a trabajar con su hijo(a) en este programa. A continuación, veremos cómo funciona el programa.

Cada lunes, les enviaré dos poemas, páginas para la familia y una hoja de lecturas en la carpeta de **Inicio rápido** de su hijo(a).

El método de **Inicio rápido** es sencillo:

Primero, lean el poema.

Después...

Dediquen unos minutos a realizar las actividades de la página para la familia. En la hoja de lecturas, les indicaré cuáles deben hacer con su hijo(a) pero, si lo desean, también podrán realizar las actividades de las otras dos secciones.

En la hoja de lecturas, anoten el tiempo que les tomó a ustedes y a su hijo(a) realizar las actividades.

Por favor, envíen la carpeta a la escuela con su hijo(a) cada lunes.

¡Que lo disfruten! Como siempre, si tienen cualquier pregunta o quieren comentarme algo acerca de su hijo(a), pueden comunicarse conmigo. ¡Juntos ayudaremos a los niños a llegar a ser hábiles y exitosos lectores!

Atentamente,

1, 2, 3, Read!

★ The *Fast Start* Routine

Fast Start combines several principles of effective reading instruction. The routine is simple:

Read to your child,
Read with your child,
Listen to your child read!

1. **Read to your child.** Sit together in a comfortable, quiet, well-lit place. Read the poem aloud to your child several times, pointing to the words as you read. You are modeling fluent reading! Learning something is difficult if we don't understand what it should look or sound like. That's why reading aloud to children is so important.

2. **Read with your child.** Read the poem aloud several times with your child. Choral reading (reading aloud together with your child) is a very supportive way to introduce a new text. Don't be concerned if your child misses a word or two.

3. **Listen to your child read.** In this step, your child reads the poem several times to you! Offer lavish praise (and help, if necessary). Like musicians or athletes, readers must practice to achieve fluency. If your child stumbles on a word when reading independently, wait a second or two and then simply say the word. As your child's fluency increases, you might even tape-record him or her!

Then do an activity or two from the family page.

Keep the atmosphere gamelike and relaxed, so that children stay engaged and enjoy the interactions. You can check off activities as you do them. You might repeat the same activity until your child seems very confident doing it.

Follow this routine at least two days in a row for each poem.

Record your time on the log sheet after each session, to share information with the teacher and to help you keep track of your sessions.

Making *Fast Start* Work for Limited-English Proficient Families

Families whose first language is not English can also participate in *Fast Start*. In order to prepare materials for them, first determine parents' or older siblings' English proficiency. The poems are very simple, so if family members can read some English, the *Fast Start* activities can proceed as with native English speakers. If family members are not proficient in reading English:

- Ask a classroom volunteer to record the poems on audiotape. Two versions of each poem will be best. The first should be slow and deliberate. The second should be a fluent rendition. Children can keep their tapes in their *Fast Start* folders. The *Fast Start* routine would then be modified: First, parent and child look at the text and listen to the taped versions of a poem several times. Then they read together and along with the taped version. Finally, the child reads the poem by him- or herself. In these instances, you may want to advise parents not to play the word games.
- Family members may be studying English themselves. See how you might help both children and their families. For example, adults might practice the *Fast Start* poems in their English classes so they can read the poems with their children at home.
- Check with the ELL teachers or tutors in your school. Because they will have knowledge about children's linguistic backgrounds, they may have more specific ideas for families. Share *Fast Start* information with the teachers or tutors. Children can practice the poems in their ELL classes. Teachers or tutors may want to play the word games with children as well.

56

Best Deal in Town

I go to the library after school
And find myself a book that's cool.
There is no charge,
The books are free.
Just how much better could it be?

—Betsy Franco

page 134

59

My Neighborhood

People move in,
People move out,
Little children play and shout.
Old people, young people,
In-between,
Make a lively neighborhood scene.

—Betsy Franco

page 140

Using the Family Pages

Here are the types of activities you'll find on the family pages. These pages are designed to help your child learn how words work and how they can be decoded. The teacher will mark the level appropriate for your child, but feel free to try activities from other sections as well.

Looking at Words and Letters

These activities help children develop basic reading and word concepts.

- Ask your child to count the lines (or words) in the poem. Ask him or her to point at each line as it is counted.
- Clap the syllables (beats) in a word. Say the words in the poem while clapping your hands. The claps correspond to the syllables in the words (for instance, *hello* has two syllables, *hel-lo*).
- Ask questions about the words, such as *How many words are in line one? Can you show me the third word in line two? Which line has the most words? Which line has the fewest words?*
- Say a letter of the alphabet. Ask your child to find all the times that a particular letter is used in the poem. Repeat for several other letters.
- Point to a word. Ask your child to tell you the letter that begins the word. Then ask him or her to tell you what letter ends the word. Repeat with several words.

Playing With Sounds

These activities help children develop basic phonics skills.

- Say two words from the poem. Ask your child to tell you if the words rhyme with one another. Repeat with several other pairs of words.
- Find a simple rhyming word (such as *pat*). Ask your child to say some words that rhyme with that word (*cat*, *sat*, *mat*). List these words on a sheet of paper. Practice reading these words.
- "Stretch" out a word from the poem (simply say it very slowly, breaking it into separate sounds, such as "bat": *buh …aaa …t*). Ask your child to tell you what word it is, or to find the word in the poem. This activity helps children hear the individual sounds in words, an important step in literacy development.
- Say two words from the poem. Ask your child if they start with the same sound. Repeat several times with other word pairs. (Choose some words that start with the same sounds and some that don't.) Later, do the same with ending sounds.

Beginning to Read

These activities reinforce phonics concepts and develop children's word recognition skills.

- Using slips of paper or index cards, make a deck of word cards. Save these in an envelope so your child can play with them independently.
- Together, select a word or two from the poem to put on the cards. After you have gathered 10 to 12 words in your word bank over several days, practice reading and playing with them. If you make a duplicate set of cards, you can play Concentration, Go Fish or Bingo.
- Ask your child to find words that rhyme (such as *man* and *can*) and list them on a sheet of paper. Ask your child to think of more words that share the letter patterns and could go on the list (*ran*, *pan*, *tan*). Write them down and have your child practice reading the list.
- Ask your child to find and circle words that:
    - have suffixes (such as *-ing*, *-ed*, *-es*)
    - have long (or short) vowel sounds
    - are compound words (longer words that contain two separate words, such as *sidewalk* or *blueberry*)
    - are people (or places, colors, and so on)
- Create a "Word Wall." Ask your child to choose several words from the poem to record on a large piece of paper or an open file folder. They can be words that were difficult, or simply words that he or she likes. Practice reading the words daily. You can write categories down on a sheet of paper (for example, words that are nouns and words that are not nouns) and have your child sort the words by the categories. Display these lists in the child's bedroom or on the refrigerator. From time to time, play games such as I Spy with your child (*I spy the word* snow, *I spy a word that starts with A, I spy a word that's the opposite of "down"*).

Dear Families,

The school year is already halfway over! Children have made lots of growth as readers this year. I know we all share the hope that this progress will continue. **Fast Start** is an important way for us to work together to support your child's growth in reading. I hope you have been able to spend ten minutes each evening with the poetry reading and activities. As a reminder:

* Have your child sit next to you. Read the poem to your child several times. Point to the words as you read.
* Ask your child to read the poem with you. Do this several times as well.
* Ask your child to read the poem several times by him- or herself. Tell your child what a great reader he or she is.
* Spend a few minutes doing the activities on the family page.
* Record each session on the log sheet. Have your child return your log sheet every Monday.

Remember:

Read **to . . .**

Read **with . . .**

Listen to your child read!

Sincerely,

Queridos familiares:

¡Ya estamos a mitad del curso escolar! Este año, los niños han hecho grandes progresos en lectura. Sé que todos compartimos la esperanza de que este progreso continuará el resto del curso. **Inicio rápido** es una manera eficaz de colaborar, Uds. y yo, para ayudar a su hijo(a) a desarrollar habilidades de lectura. Espero que hayan podido dedicar 10 minutos cada noche a realizar las lecturas de poesía y las actividades. Recuerden:

* Siéntense junto a su hijo(a). Léanle el poema varias veces. Vayan señalando las palabras con el dedo a medida que lean.
* Pídanle a su hijo(a) que lea el poema con Uds. Repitan también la lectura conjunta varias veces.
* Pidan a su hijo(a) que lea varias veces el poema solo(a). Halágenlo(a) por lo bien que está leyendo.
* Dediquen unos minutos a realizar las actividades de la página para la familia.
* Anoten cada sesión del programa en la hoja de lecturas. Envíenla cada lunes a la escuela con su hijo(a).

Recuerden:

Leer **a . . .**

Leer **con . . .**

¡Escuchar a su hijo(a) leer!

Atentamente,

Fast Start in the Classroom

Introducing Fast Start to Students

Foster children's enthusiasm for the program with a classroom introduction:

* Explain the basics of the program and show children what they will be doing at home each evening. A demonstration with you playing the role of a parent will work well. Demonstrate at least one activity from each category.
* Answer children's questions about the program. Some may wonder if an older sibling, grandparent, or babysitter can do *Fast Start* with them. *Fast Start* works fine with a variety of people playing the parent role; consistent practice is the most important feature!
* Remind children to return their log sheets every Monday.
* Short, frequent classroom discussions about children's *Fast Start* experiences will also keep enthusiasm high.

Take a little classroom time each week (or even each day) to share the poem of the week. Classroom follow-up keeps children's enthusiasm high and reinforces their learning. Children enjoy sharing their *Fast Start* experiences and are proud that they can read the poems successfully!

You can build upon and support what's happening at home in five easy steps:

1. Write the poem of the week on chart paper, a flip chart, or a pocket chart, and display.
2. Have children read chorally (all together) or have different groups read different sections of the poem as you (or a child volunteer) track the print with your finger or a pointer.
3. Divide the class into pairs and have children read the poem several times to their partners.
4. Do a few of the more challenging wordplay activities.
5. Add some words from the poems to class word walls.

Managing *Fast Start*: Helpful Hints

Managing the program is easy, and you'll naturally develop a management system that works for you. Here are some tips:

- ☑ Remind children to return the completed log sheets to you each Monday. You can use these to track participation. You might suggest that families use a magnet to keep the sheet on their refrigerators. To avoid being overwhelmed by paperwork, review returned log sheets once a month.

- ☑ Use the poems in any order that works for you (see pages 18–19). Many teachers follow the presentation in the book. Because wordplay activities are differentiated, all children can read the same poems at the same time, which facilitates classroom follow-up.

- ☑ Most families sustain their *Fast Start* involvement because they enjoy it. Families see children's growth, and this motivates them to continue with the program. You can also provide small incentives (see bookmarks on page 20) occasionally to keep their interest high. Other incentives, such as pencils, stickers, a chance to have lunch with you, or an opportunity to read to the principal may also work well. An end-of-the-year certificate is provided on page 21.

- ☑ If you prepare a classroom newsletter, occasionally include articles about *Fast Start*. You might want to feature children's comments about how much they enjoy *Fast Start* or remind families about their critical role in their children's learning. You can write about solutions to any problems or concerns related to *Fast Start* as well.

- ☑ Surveys and interviews are the easiest ways to get feedback about the program. Page 23 is a reproducible survey for families. Send the family survey home with children toward the end of the school year. Analyze responses to these surveys by noting the number of people who gave a particular response as well as any comments they provided. You can also compare responses by groups: families who were consistently involved in *Fast Start* versus those who were inconsistently involved.

- ☑ Calling a few individual families each week is a good way to maintain family involvement and answer families' questions or concerns about *Fast Start*.

- ☑ Drop a note home occasionally to remind families to read the *Fast Start* poems with their children.

Fast Start Log

For ______________________________ Week of ____________________

Please work on the activities in the section labeled:

☐ **Looking at Words and Letters** ☐ **Playing With Sounds** ☐ **Beginning to Read**

Day	Poem	Time	Comments
Monday			
Tuesday			
Wednesday			
Thursday			
Friday			
Saturday			
Sunday			

The Poems

You can use the *Fast Start* poems in several ways. As listed in the book, the poems correspond to the seasons and the easiest poems appear in the beginning of the book. The lists that follow may also be helpful as you decide how to use the poems. The first two lists show the word families and phonics elements present in the poems. The third list shows common themes. Spend a few minutes looking at the poems and decide what might work best in your classroom reading program.

Word Families

Word Family	Poems
-ack*	4, 44
-ake*	27, 30
-alk	57
-all	7, 50
-ame	45, 48
-an*	1
-ap*	46
-at*	15
-ay*	3, 31, 32, 39
-e, -ee	14, 22
-eat	46
-eck	41
-eep	8, 20, 26, 32, 33, 44
-eet	30, 46, 49
-ell*	37
-er	52, 60
-ick*	5, 41, 52
-ide	57
-ight*	50
-iggle	57
-ike	31, 36, 47
-ile	29
-ill*	34
-ing*	19, 31, 38, 42
-ive (as in *hive*)	18
-o (as in *so*)	18
-ock*	5, 11
-old	54
-ong	31
-ook	31, 35
-ool	56
-oon	17, 48
-op*	28, 57
-orn	20
-ose	10, 55
-ounce	57
-ound	36, 48
-ouse	29
-out*	2, 59
-ow* (as in *row*)	25, 32, 42, 58
-ow (as in *cow*)	44, 58
-ub	40
-ud	51
-ump	57
-y* (as in *try*)	50

*= most common word families

Sounds

Sounds	Poems
Short & Long A	1, 3, 4, 7, 15, 27, 30, 31, 32, 39, 44, 45, 46, 48, 50, 57
Short & Long E	8, 12, 14, 20, 22, 26, 30, 32, 33, 37, 41, 44, 46, 49, 52, 53, 60
Short & Long I	5, 13, 17, 18, 19, 26, 29, 31, 34, 36, 38, 41, 42, 47, 50, 52, 57
Short & Long O	5, 10, 11, 16, 17, 18, 20, 25, 28, 29, 31, 32, 42, 49, 50, 54, 55, 58
Short & Long U	40, 51, 57

Themes

Theme	Poems
All About Me	6, 10, 13, 19, 35, 37, 45, 46, 54, 56, 60
Animals	2, 3, 5, 8, 12, 15, 17, 20, 21, 33, 40, 41, 42, 44, 52, 57
Basic Concepts	5, 6, 11, 30, 31, 48, 50
Birds & Bugs	2, 9, 38, 41, 57
Food	1, 14, 23, 24, 27
Health	19, 37, 45
Movement & Travel	5, 13, 30, 36, 39, 46, 47, 49, 57
Numbers	6, 14, 18
Nursery Rhymes	1, 3, 5, 7, 8, 9, 15, 16, 17, 20, 21, 22, 23, 24, 29, 38
Outdoors	18, 25, 26, 28, 30, 32, 34, 36, 39, 47, 55, 58, 60
Plants	14, 58
Reading	35, 56
Songs & Games	1, 2, 4, 12, 26
Weather & Seasons	25, 28, 32, 43, 51

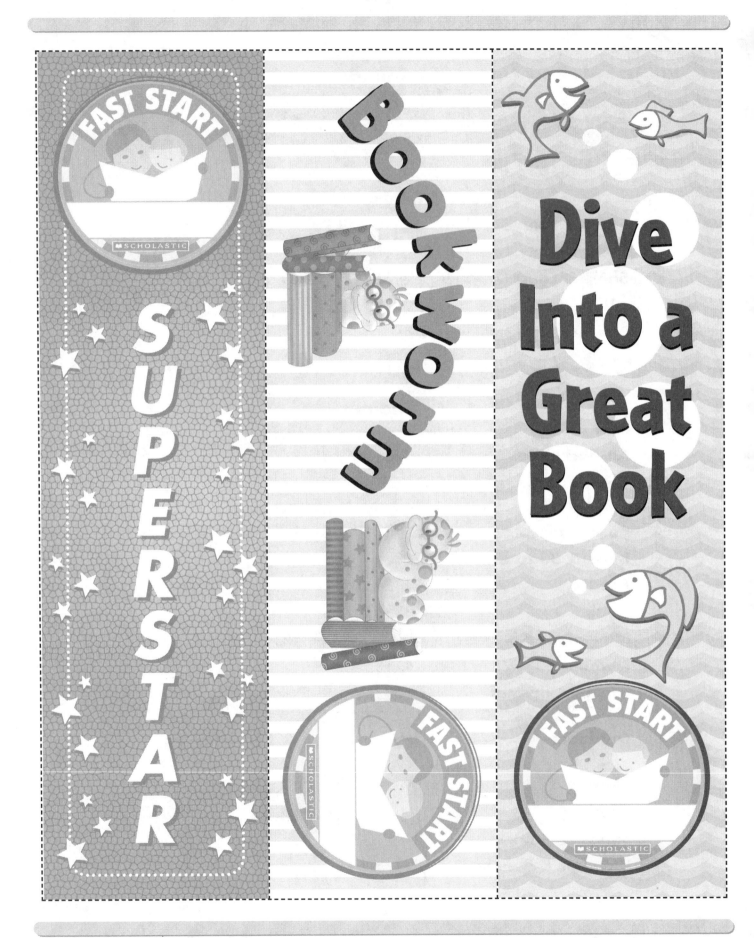

FAST START
SCHOLASTIC
SUPERSTAR
BOOKWORM
Dive Into a Great Book
FAST START
SCHOLASTIC
FAST START
SCHOLASTIC

This is to certify that

____

has completed

FAST START

for Early Readers

Date ______________________________

Signed ______________________________

Congratulations!

Assessing Children's Progress

It's relatively easy to assess the impact that *Fast Start* has on your students as readers. Here are some plans for evaluating their reading achievement and for assessing children's (see below) and families' (see page 23) opinions about *Fast Start*.

Most schools, districts, and states already mandate periodic tests of reading growth. The easiest way to evaluate the impact of *Fast Start* is to use the standardized testing results you already have. Simply divide the children in your class into three groups: those who participated regularly and actively in *Fast Start*, those whose participation was more sporadic, and those who did not participate at all. Make a chart for each group:

Name	September Results	May Results	Change (+/–)

- Analyzing data in this way will allow you to look at the growth children show over the year. You can compare results for children at different levels of *Fast Start* participation.
- Spreadsheet software can also be useful. Many programs can calculate averages and other helpful statistics.
- Share positive results with families. Families may be more eager to continue their participation in the program if they know their time is paying off!

Three-Minute Reading Assessments (Rasinski & Padak, Scholastic, 2005) is a program that allows you to quickly assess children's growth in word recognition, fluency, and comprehension—three keys to reading success. Assess children's reading three or four times a year in order to document growth in these key areas.

Children's Interview Questions

- Did you like reading the poetry? Why?
- Did you like the wordplay activities? Why?
- Who read the poems and played the games with you? Did he or she enjoy this? How do you know?
- Do you think the poems and activities have made you a better reader? Why?
- How can I make *Fast Start* better for next year's class?

Dear Families:

Now that the school year is almost over, I would like your opinion of the **Fast Start** program, the nightly poetry reading and word play activities you have been doing with your child. Your feedback will help me refine the program for next year's class! Please use the back of the sheet for your comments.

Sincerely,

____

FAST START SURVEY

Parent's Name ______________________ Child's Name ______________________

1. Did your child like the *Fast Start* sessions?
_____ yes _____ somewhat _____ no
Please explain.

2. Did you enjoy the *Fast Start* sessions?
_____ yes _____ somewhat _____ no
Please explain.

3. Did your child enjoy the poems?
_____ yes _____ somewhat _____ no
Please explain.

4. Did your child enjoy the word play activities?
_____ yes _____ somewhat _____ no
Please explain.

5. Do you think *Fast Start* has made a difference in your child's reading?
_____ yes _____ somewhat _____ no
Please explain.

6. What problems did you have with *Fast Start*?

7. How can I make the program better?

Queridos familiares: Ahora que el curso va llegando a su final, me gustaría saber su opinión sobre **Inicio rápido**, el programa de lecturas de poesía y actividades de juegos de palabras que han estado realizando cada noche con su hijo(a). Conocer sus opiniones sobre el programa me permitirá mejorarlo para la clase del próximo curso. Haga uso de la parte trasera de esta pagina

Atentamente,

____

ENCUESTA SOBRE *INICIO RAPIDO*

Nombre del padre o la madre ______________________ Nombre del niño(a) ______________________

1. ¿A su hijo(a) le gustaron las sesiones del programa Inicio rápido?
_____ sí _____ más o menos _____ no
Por favor, explique su respuesta.

2. ¿Disfrutó Ud. las sesiones del programa Inicio rápido?
_____ sí _____ más o menos _____ no
Por favor, explique su respuesta.

3. ¿Le gustaron a su hijo(a) los poemas?
_____ sí _____ más o menos _____ no
Por favor, explique su respuesta.

4. ¿Disfrutó su hijo(a) las actividades de juegos de palabras?
_____ sí _____ más o menos _____ no
Por favor, explique su respuesta.

5. ¿Cree que el programa Inicio rápido ha ayu dado eficazmente a su hijo(a) a aprender a leer?
_____ sí _____ más o menos _____ no
Por favor, explique su respuesta.

6. ¿Qué problemas tuvo con el programa?

7. ¿Qué me sugiere que haga para mejorar el programa?

1

Pat-a-Cake

Pat-a-cake, pat-a-cake,
Baker's man,
Bake me a cake
As fast as you can.
Pat it and prick it
And mark it with a T.
Put it in the oven
For Tommy and me.

Pat-a-Cake

★ 1 ★

Looking at Words and Letters

☐ **1.** Ask your child how many lines are in the poem. Invite him or her to number the lines.

☐ **2.** Ask, *Which is the longest line? How many words does it have?*

☐ **3.** Ask your child to find uppercase *B*. Say, *Which word is* Baker*? Circle it. Which word is "Bake"? Underline it.*

☐ **4.** Have your child point to the first and last word in the poem, and then count all the words.

Playing With Sounds

☐ **1.** Say, *I'll say two words. You tell me if they rhyme:*

man, can **can, cake** **cake, bake**

☐ **2.** Say, *Listen while I stretch out the sounds in these words. You tell me the words:*

p . . . aaa . . . t (pat)
m . . . aaa . . . nnn (man)
b . . . aay . . . k (bake)

☐ **3.** Say, *I'll say two words. You tell me if they start the same way:*

man, mark **cake, bake** **pat, put**

Beginning to Read

☐ **1.** Write the following words on index cards or small slips of paper. Ask your child to sort them into two groups: long "a" words and short "a" words.

pat, man, fast, and (short "a") *cake, bake, baker's* (long "a")

☐ **2.** Ask your child to circle the words in the poem that start with the sound "b." Repeat with "p."

☐ **3.** Write the word *man* on a sheet of paper. Ask your child to name other words that rhyme with *man* (*Ann, ban, can, Dan, fan, pan, ran, tan*). Together, write these new words.

☐ **4.** Together, choose two or three words from the poem. Add them to your word wall and practice these words daily. Or, add them to your child's word bank (a collection of words on cards, one word per card).

Itsy Bitsy Spider

The itsy bitsy spider
Climbed up the water spout.
Down came the rain
And washed the spider out.
Out came the sun
And dried up all the rain.
And the itsy bitsy spider
Climbed up the spout again.

Itsy Bitsy Spider

★ 2 ★

Looking at Words and Letters

☐ **1.** Ask your child to find the shortest line in the poem and then count the words in that line.

☐ **2.** Ask your child to find and underline each "s" in the poem.

☐ **3.** Ask, *What is this poem about?*

Playing With Sounds

☐ **1.** Say, *Let's change the word* rain. *What if we added "t" to the beginning? What word would that be?* (train) *What if the word started with "p"?* (pain) *What if it started with "spr"?* (sprain)

☐ **2.** Say, *I will stretch out some words. You tell me what they are:*

rrr…aaay…nnn (rain)
c…aaay…mmm (came)

☐ **3.** Say, *Now you try it. Stretch these words out:* sun, spider.

Beginning to Read

☐ **1.** Ask your child to name some words that rhyme with *sun*. Write them as your child says them. To start off, offer some beginning sounds: "b," "f."

☐ **2.** Say, *Do these words end with the same sound?*

itsy, bitsy   **down, came**   **and, rain**   **spout, out**

☐ **3.** Ask your child to draw a picture of the poem, then tell you what it is about.

☐ **4.** Write *spout* on a sheet of paper. Point out the letters *-out*. Brainstorm, write, and read other words that rhyme and explain that all these words belong to the *-out* word family.

☐ **5.** Together, choose two or three words from the poem. Add them to your word wall and practice these words daily. Or add them to your child's word bank (a collection of words on cards, one word per card).

Mary Had a Little Lamb

**Mary had a little lamb,
Its fleece was white as snow.
And everywhere that Mary went,
The lamb was sure to go.**

**It followed her to school one day,
Which was against the rules.
It made the children laugh and play
To see a lamb at school.**

Mary Had a Little Lamb

★ 3 ★

★ Looking at Words and Letters

☐ **1.** Ask your child to count the words in the first line. Then ask your child to circle each word.

☐ **2.** Say, *Circle the first word in line two; now circle the last word in line two.* Repeat for line three.

☐ **3.** Say, *Look at these words. What letter starts them?* (point to *little, lamb, laugh*). Have your child practice writing lowercase *l* and uppercase *L*.

★ Playing With Sounds

☐ **1.** Say, *I'll say two words. Clap your hands if they rhyme:*

day, play **see, school** **snow, go**

☐ **2.** Say, *Think about the word* day. *What other words rhyme with it? You say them, and I'll write them down.* (bay, hay, jay, lay, pay, ray, say, stay, tray, way)

☐ **3.** Say, *I'll stretch some words. You tell me what the word is:*

l...a...m (lamb)
r...oo...l...s (rules)
sch...oo...l (school)

☐ **4.** Ask your child to find and circle the word *Mary* each time it is used in the poem.

★ Beginning to Read

☐ **1.** Say, *I'll say a word. You say one that rhymes. I say,* white. *You say...*(bright, night, bite, and so on). Repeat with *snow, play, see.*

☐ **2.** Write these words on slips of paper: *snow, go, to, one.* Ask your child to pick out the two words with a long "o." (*snow, go*)

☐ **3.** Tap or clap the beats in the poem. Then ask your child to join you. Finally, ask your child, "How many beats are in the word *snow?* (1) *children?* (2) *laugh?* (1) *everywhere?* (3)"

☐ **4.** Write *day* on a sheet of paper. Point out the letters *-ay*. Together, brainstorm, write, and read other words that rhyme and list them on a sheet of paper.

☐ **5.** Together, choose two or three words from the poem. Add them to your word wall and practice these words daily. Or add them to your child's word bank (a collection of words on cards, one word per card).

Miss Mary Mack

Miss Mary Mack
All dressed in black,
With a big red bow
In the middle of the back.
She carried her lunch
In a purple pack,
And her high-heeled shoes
Went clickety-clack.

Miss Mary Mack

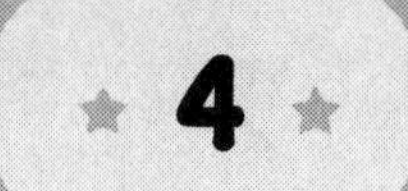

Looking at Words and Letters

☐ **1.** Ask your child to circle the words that start with "b."

☐ **2.** Say, *I will say two words. Clap your hands if they rhyme:*

big, bow **back, sack** **black, sack**

☐ **3.** Ask your child to find a line in the poem that has two "m" words and then circle them. Repeat with "p" words.

Playing With Sounds

☐ **1.** Say the word *Mack*. Ask your child to name some words that rhyme with it (*back, clack, pack, sack, track*). On blank paper, list the words.

☐ **2.** Say, *I'll stretch some words out. You tell me which word I'm saying:*

s…a…k (sack)
cl…a…k (clack)
b…a…k (back)

☐ **3.** Say, *I'll say two words. Raise your hand if they start the same:*

Mary, middle **clack, back** **clickety, clack**

Beginning to Read

☐ **1.** Write these words on index cards or little slips of paper: *pat, cake, man, bake, rain, lamb, made, Mack, black, pack*. Ask your child to sort the words into two categories: long "a" (*cake, bake, rain, made*) and short "a" (*pat, man, lamb, Mack, black, pack*).

☐ **2.** Using the same word cards, ask your child to group rhyming words together. Then ask your child to add words to each group.

☐ **3.** Ask your child to find and circle the color words in the poem.

☐ **4.** Write *back* on a sheet of paper. Point out the *-ack* word family. Together, brainstorm, write, and read other words that belong to the *-ack* word family (*back, pack, sack*).

☐ **5.** Together, choose two or three words from the poem. Add them to your word wall and practice these words daily. Or add them to your child's word bank (a collection of words on cards, one word per card).

Hickory Dickory Dock

Hickory, dickory, dock,
The mouse ran up the clock.
The clock struck one,
The mouse ran down,
Hickory, dickory, dock!

Hickory Dickory Dock

5

Looking at Words and Letters

☐ **1.** Ask your child how many words are in the first line. Ask your child to point to each word. Repeat with line two.

☐ **2.** Ask your child to find and underline each "k" in the poem.

☐ **3.** Say, *The word* mouse *is in the poem twice. Can you find and circle* mouse?

Playing With Sounds

☐ **1.** Say, *I will say two words. Clap your hands if they rhyme:*

one, down **dock, clock** **hickory, dickory**

☐ **2.** Say, *I'm thinking of a word that rhymes with* dock *and tells us the time* (clock). *We use a key to do this to a door* (lock). *This is a big group of birds in the sky* (flock).

☐ **3.** Ask your child to stretch out the words *clock, block, flock.*

Beginning to Read

☐ **1.** Ask your child to circle the short "o" words in the poem. (*dock, clock*)

☐ **2.** Have your child illustrate the poem and describe to you what he or she has drawn.

☐ **3.** Say, *Change the first sound of* dock *to "l." What's the word?* (lock). *Now change the first sound to "bl"* (block). *Now to "fl"* (flock).

☐ **4.** Write *dock* on a sheet of paper. Point out the -*ock* word family. Together, brainstorm, write, and read words that rhyme with *dock.* (*block, shock, knock*)

☐ **5.** Together, choose two or three words from the poem. Add them to your word wall and practice these words daily. Or add them to your child's word bank (a collection of words on cards, one word per card).

Fingerplay

Ten fingers,
Ten toes,
Two eyes, two ears, two lips,
One nose!

Fingers tickle,
Toes can wiggle,
Eyes can twinkle,
Nose can wrinkle.

Ten fingers,
Ten toes,
Two eyes, two ears, two lips,
One nose!

—Helen H. Moore

Fingerplay

Looking at Words and Letters

☐ **1.** Ask your child to find and circle two lines that are exactly the same, then find and underline two more lines that are exactly the same.

☐ **2.** Ask, *What is the longest line in the poem? How many words does it have?*

☐ **3.** Ask your child to circle all the uppercase *T*'s, then draw boxes around the lowercase *t*'s.

Playing With Sounds

☐ **1.** Say, *Let's clap or tap the beats in the poem together. Then ask, How many beats do you hear in* ten? *in* tickle? *in* fingers? *in* toes?

☐ **2.** Say, *I will stretch out some words. You tell me the words*:

n...oh...zuh (nose)
l...ih...ps (lips)
wh...ig...ell (wiggle)

☐ **3.** Say these words in pairs. Ask your child to raise a hand if they start the same:

ten, two **can, fan** **finger, fan** **wiggle, wrinkle** **toes, nose**

Now repeat the pairs of words. Ask your child to raise a hand if they rhyme.

Beginning to Read

☐ **1.** Say, *Find and circle the number words. Write the numerals that the words stand for.*

☐ **2.** Ask your child to find the words that name parts of the body and to draw a square around each one.

☐ **3.** Ask your child which stanza (a group of four lines) has more words—the first one or the second one. Then ask which stanza has more syllables or beats—the first one or the second one.

☐ **4.** Write *lip* on a sheet of paper. Point out the *-ip* word family. Together, brainstorm, write, and read other words that rhyme and belong to the *-ip* word family.

☐ **5.** Together, choose two or three words from the poem. Add them to your word wall and practice these daily. Or add them to your child's word bank (a collection of words on cards, one word per card).

Humpty Dumpty

Humpty Dumpty sat on a wall,
Humpty Dumpty had a great fall.
All the king's horses
And all the king's men
Couldn't put Humpty together again!

Humpty Dumpty

Looking at Words and Letters

☐ **1.** Ask, *Which lines have the most words? How many words do they each have?*

☐ **2.** Ask, *Which line has the fewest words? How many words does it have?*

☐ **3.** Ask your child to circle the words that have two *l*'s in a row. (*wall, fall, all*)

Playing With Sounds

☐ **1.** Say, *I'll say two words. Clap your hands if they rhyme:*

again, men **all, wall** **horses, Humpty**

☐ **2.** Say, *I'll say a word, then you say one that rhymes:* sat. *(mat, hat)* Repeat with *king, wall, men.*

☐ **3.** Say, *I'm going to stretch some words into their separate sounds. Tell me the words I am stretching:*

h...aaa...d (had)
a...nn...d (and)
p...uu...t (put)

Beginning to Read

☐ **1.** Ask your child to circle the words that name living things.

☐ **2.** Say, *We'll start with* all. *What's the word if we put "b" in the beginning?* (ball) Repeat with "f," "sm," "h," "m," "t," "w."

☐ **3.** Put the *–all* words from the exercise above on index cards or small slips of paper. Write each word on two cards. Turn them over, and play Concentration together.

☐ **4.** Write *wall* on a sheet of paper. Point out the *-all* word family. Together, brainstorm, write, and read other words that rhyme and belong to the word family.

☐ **5.** Together, choose two or three words from the poem. Add them to your word wall and practice these words daily. Or add them to your child's word bank (a collection of words on cards, one word per card).

Little Bo Peep

Little Bo Peep
Has lost her sheep,
And doesn't know where to find them.
Leave them alone,
And they'll come home,
Wagging their tails behind them.

Little Bo Peep

★ 8 ★

Looking at Words and Letters

☐ **1.** Ask your child to find and circle the *t*'s.

☐ **2.** Ask your child to find and circle the two lines in the poem that have only three words.

☐ **3.** Say, *I'll say two words. You raise your hand if they begin the same:*

little, lost **peep, bo** **lost, leave**

☐ **4.** Ask your child to count all the words in the poem.

☐ **5.** Ask your child to point to the top, then the bottom, of the poem.

Playing With Sounds

☐ **1.** Say, *Listen while I clap (or tap) the beats of the poem. Now let's clap (or tap) the beats of the poem together.*

☐ **2.** Ask your child how many beats are in these words: *little* (2), *lost* (1), *leave* (1), *wagging* (2).

☐ **3.** Say, *I'll say two words. Clap your hands if they rhyme:*

alone, them **sheep, peep** **come, home**

Beginning to Read

☐ **1.** Ask your child to find and circle words with a long "o". (*Bo, know, alone, home*)

☐ **2.** Say, *I'll say a word. You tell me the last sound in it:* peep, lost, them, tails.

☐ **3.** Ask your child to find the words with two syllables or beats and to underline them. (*little, doesn't, alone, wagging, behind*)

☐ **4.** Write *sheep* on a sheet of paper. Point out the *-eep* word family. Together, brainstorm, write, and read other words that rhyme and belong to the word family.

☐ **5.** Together, choose two or three words from the poem. Add them to your word wall and practice these words daily. Or add them to your child's word bank (a collection of words on cards, one word per card).

Little Miss Muffet

Little Miss Muffet
Sat on a tuffet
Eating her curds and whey.
Along came a spider
And sat down beside her
And frightened Miss Muffet away!

Little Miss Muffet

9

Looking at Words and Letters

☐ **1.** Ask your child to find and circle three uppercase *A*'s and three lowercase *a*'s.

☐ **2.** Ask, *How many words are in the first line of the poem? How about the last line? Which line has more words?*

☐ **3.** Have your child point to the first line of the poem, then underline the first word and last word. Repeat with the last line.

☐ **4.** Ask your child to point to the first word in the poem and then to the last word.

Playing With Sounds

☐ **1.** Say, *Let's say words that rhyme with* sat. *I'll say the first sound; you tell me the word*: "b," "f," "m," "p," "th." (*bat, fat, mat, pat, that*)

☐ **2.** Ask your child why these words belong together: *Muffet, tuffet* (they rhyme); *curds, came* (they start the same); *Miss, Muffet* (they start the same and they are both part of the girl's name).

☐ **3.** Take turns stretching out words and guessing what they are: *sat, and, miss, beside, spider, eating.*

Beginning to Read

☐ **1.** Ask your child to circle the words with one syllable or beat. (*Miss, sat, on, a, her, curds, and, whey, came, a, and, sat, down, her, and, Miss*)

☐ **2.** Ask your child to underline the words in the poem with two syllables or beats. (*Little, Muffet, tuffet, eating, along, spider, beside, frightened, Muffet, away*)

☐ **3.** Say, *Take the "c" off* came. *Start with "g." What's the word?* (game) Repeat with "bl," "s," "t," and "fl."

☐ **4.** Ask your child to find and underline the words *little, sat, tuffet,* and *spider.*

☐ **5.** Together, choose two or three words from the poem. Add them to your word wall and practice these words daily. Or add them to your child's word bank (a collection of words on cards, one word per card).

I'm Me!

In the mirror
What do I see?
Someone special,
That is me!

My eyes, my ears,
My lips, my nose.
No one's looks are
Just like those!

—Meish Goldish

I'm Me!

Looking at Words and Letters

☐ **1.** Ask your child to count the lines in the poem.

☐ **2.** Say, *Underline the first word in the poem. Now underline the last word in the poem.*

☐ **3.** Ask your child to find and circle the words that start with *M, m.* Have him or her practice writing the letter *M, m.*

Playing With Sounds

☐ **1.** Say, *I'll say two words. Clap your hands if they rhyme:*

see, me **see, someone** **nose, those**

☐ **2.** Ask your child which word doesn't belong in each group of three. Ask your child for reasons.

special, me, my **like, lips, is**

☐ **3.** Say, *Let's take the "s" off the word* see. *What if it started with "b"? What is the new word?* (be or bee) Repeat with "fr," "m," and "sh."

Beginning to Read

☐ **1.** Ask your child to underline words that name body parts.

☐ **2.** Invite your child to draw a picture of him- or herself and label *eyes, ears, lips,* and *nose,* as in the poem.

☐ **3.** Ask your child to find and circle the words that have two syllables or beats. (*mirror, someone, special*)

☐ **4.** Write *see* and *me* on a sheet of paper. Point out the word endings *-ee* and *-e.* Together, brainstorm, write, and read other words that rhyme and belong to these word families.

☐ **5.** Together, choose two or three words from the poem. Add them to your word wall and practice these words daily. Or add them to your child's word bank (a collection of words on cards, one word per card).

11

What Do You Need?

To build a house
You need a block.
To tell the time
You need a clock.
To open a door
You need to knock.
To sail a ship
You need a dock.
And to cover your foot,
You need a sock.
Block, clock,
Tick tock,
Knock, dock
Sock!

—Helen O'Reilly

What Do You Need?

11

Looking at Words and Letters

☐ **1.** Ask your child to count the words in the first and last lines. Say, *Which line has more words, the first or the last?*

☐ **2.** Ask your child to underline the lines with four words.

☐ **3.** Point to the word *to* in the poem. Say, *Circle the word* to *in other places in the poem.*

Playing With Sounds

☐ **1.** Say, *Tell me if these words rhyme with block*: house, clock, time, door, knock.

☐ **2.** Say, *Here are some riddles. All the answers will rhyme with* block.

I am a stone. (rock)
You put me on your foot. (sock)
I am a big bunch of birds flying in the sky. (flock)
I tell you the time. (clock)

☐ **3.** Say, *Clap your hands if the words start with the same sound:*

tell, time	**dock, knock**	**door, dock**
sail, sock	**house, mouse**	**sail, time**

Now I'll say the same pairs of words again. Raise your hand if they rhyme.

Beginning to Read

☐ **1.** Ask your child to circle the words in the poem that are things you can touch.

☐ **2.** Make two word cards for each of these words and play Concentration: *block, clock, knock, sock, dock.*

☐ **3.** Write *clock* on a sheet of paper. Point out the *-ock* word family. Together, brainstorm, write, and read other words that rhyme and belong to the word family.

☐ **4.** Say, *Let's start with tick. Change the beginning to "st." What's the word?* (stick) *Now change the beginning to "s." What's the word?* (sick) *Now change the middle to short "o." What's the word?* (sock) *Now change the beginning to "t." What's the word?* (tock)

☐ **5.** Together, choose two or three words from the poem. Add them to your word wall and practice these words daily. Or add them to your child's word bank (a collection of words on cards, one word per card).

This Little Piggy

This little piggy went to market,
This little piggy stayed home.
This little piggy had roast beef,
This little piggy had none.
And this little piggy cried
"Wee, wee, wee!"
All the way home.

This Little Piggy

12

Looking at Words and Letters

☐ **1.** Ask your child how many words are in the first line of the poem. How about the second line?

☐ **2.** Ask your child to find and circle the uppercase *T*'s. Repeat with the lowercase *t*'s.

☐ **3.** Show your child the word *little* in the title. Say, *Look for this word in the poem and underline it. How many can you find?*

Playing With Sounds

☐ **1.** Say, *Let's clap the syllables or beats as we read the poem.*

☐ **2.** Say, *How many syllables or beats do you hear in these words? this* (1), *little* (2), *piggy* (2), *market* (2)

☐ **3.** Say, *I'll say a word. You stretch it out:*

market (*mmm...ar...ket*)
home (*hh...oh...m*)
little (*l...itt...ell*)
way (*w...a...y*)

Beginning to Read

☐ **1.** Ask your child to find the words with two syllables, or beats, and to draw boxes around them. (*little, piggy, market*)

☐ **2.** Ask your child to circle the words that are places.

☐ **3.** Ask your child to underline the words in the poem with long vowel sounds. (*piggy, stayed, home, roast, beef, cried, wee, way*)

☐ **4.** Ask your child to find these words and put a box around them: *this, piggy, market, way.*

☐ **5.** Together, choose two or three words from the poem. Add them to your word wall and practice these words daily. Or add them to your child's word bank (a collection of words on cards, one word per card).

The Lesson

I splash, I flop,
I tread, I hop,
My arms go in a spin
My legs are kicking up and down
Then, suddenly! I swim.

—Jane W. Krows

The Lesson

13

Looking at Words and Letters

☐ **1.** Ask your child to find the uppercase *I*'s. Then ask your child to find lowercase *i*'s.

☐ **2.** Say, *Two lines start with* I. *How many words are in each of those lines?*

☐ **3.** Say, *Two lines start with* My. *How many words are in each of those lines?*

Playing With Sounds

☐ **1.** Say, *Let's think of words that rhyme with* hop. *You tell them to me, and I'll write them down.*

☐ **2.** Say, *Here are some riddles. Answers will rhyme with* spin.

I am the opposite of out. (in)
I am the opposite of fat. (thin)
I am the opposite of lose. (win)

☐ **3.** Say, *Listen while I stretch these words out:*

sp…la…sh (splash)
tr…eh…d (tread)

Now you try it:

spin (sp…ih…n)
swim (sw…ih…m)

Beginning to Read

☐ **1.** Ask your child to illustrate the poem and tell you about his or her picture.

☐ **2.** Say, *Let's start with* hop. *Change the first sound to "st." What's the word? Now change the first sound to "t." What's the word? Now change the first sound to "fl." What's the word?*

☐ **3.** Write *hop* on a sheet of paper. Point out the -*op* word family. Together, brainstorm, write, and read other words that rhyme and belong to the word family.

☐ **4.** Together, choose two or three words from the poem. Add them to your word wall and practice these words daily. Or add them to your child's word bank (a collection of words on cards, one word per card).

Apples Three

Fresh picked apples
From a tree
One for you
And one for me
One for teacher
That makes three
Apples picked
From an apple tree

—Monica Kulling

Apples Three

★ Looking at Words and Letters

☐ **1.** Ask your child to circle all the uppercase *A*'s, then the lowercase *a*'s. Invite him or her to practice writing the letter *A, a*.

☐ **2.** Ask your child to find and underline all the lines with three words.

☐ **3.** Say, *Draw boxes around words that end in -ee. Now draw boxes around words that end in* e. Say the words for your child. Say, *Listen to the words. Do they sound the same?*

★ Playing With Sounds

☐ **1.** Say, *I will stretch out some words. You tell me what they are.*

t...r...ee (tree)
th...r...ee (three)
th...a...t (that)

☐ **2.** Say, *Now you try stretching out some words:* fresh, from, for.

☐ **3.** Say, *Clap your hands if the words start with the same sound:*

fresh, from **tree, me** **and, apples**

★ Beginning to Read

☐ **1.** Say, *Why do these words belong together?*

One, three (both are numbers) **you, me** (both name people) **me, tree** (both end in long *e*)

☐ **2.** Ask your child to circle the number words in the poem and to write the numerals.

☐ **3.** Ask your child to underline three words in the poem that have the long "e" sound.

☐ **4.** Write *tree* and *me* on a sheet of paper. Point out the *-ee* and *-e* word families. Together, brainstorm, write, and read other words that rhyme and belong to these word families.

☐ **5.** Together, choose two or three words from the poem. Add them to your word wall and practice these words daily. Or add them to your child's word bank (a collection of words on cards, one word per card).

Old Mother Hubbard

Old Mother Hubbard went to the cupboard,
To give her poor dog a bone.
But when she got there, the cupboard was bare,
And so the poor dog had none.

She went to the baker's to buy him some bread,
And when she got back, the poor dog was fed.
She went to the hatter's to buy him a hat,
And when she came back . . .
He was feeding the cat!

Old Mother Hubbard

Looking at Words and Letters

☐ **1.** Ask your child to underline words that begin with "b." Invite him or her to practice writing the letter B, b.

☐ **2.** Ask your child to circle words that end with "d." Invite him or her to practice writing the letter D, d.

☐ **3.** Show your child the word *dog* in the poem. Say, *Can you find this word in other places in the poem?*

☐ **4.** Ask your child to count the words in the first and last lines.

Playing With Sounds

☐ **1.** Say, *I will stretch some words out. You tell me what they are:*
br…eh…d (bread)
b…a…k (back)
b…oh…n (bone)

☐ **2.** Say, *Guess the answers. They will rhyme with* back. *Trains go on me.* (track) *I am another word for* bag. (sack or pack)

☐ **3.** Say, *Help me decide if these words rhyme with* old: gold, poor, bold, dog, told.

Beginning to Read

☐ **1.** Ask your child to circle the words that name living things.

☐ **2.** Say, *Why do these words go together?*

dog, cat **hat, cat** **baker's, bread**

☐ **3.** Put these words on index cards or small slips of paper. Ask your child to group them into two piles: long "o" and short "o." Words: *old, mother, dog, bone, so, got.*

☐ **4.** Write *bread* and *fed* on a sheet of paper. Point out the word families *-ead (head, dead)* and *-ed (bed, red, Ted, wed).* Together, brainstorm, write, and read other words that rhyme and belong to the word families. Help your child remember the spellings for the various words you make.

☐ **5.** Together, choose two or three words from the poem. Add them to your word wall and practice these words daily. Or add them to your child's word bank (a collection of words on cards, one word per card).

The Old Woman Who Lived in a Shoe

There was an old woman
Who lived in a shoe.
She had so many children,
She didn't know what to do.

She gave them some broth
Along with some bread,
Then hugged them all soundly
And sent them to bed.

The Old Woman Who Lived in a Shoe

16

Looking at Words and Letters

- ☐ **1.** Say, *I will point to three words. You tell me what letter each one starts with:* woman, was, many.
- ☐ **2.** Ask your child to count the words in the first line of the poem. Then ask your child to circle the first word and the last word.
- ☐ **3.** Ask your child to find the last line of the poem and to underline the second word in that line.

Playing With Sounds

- ☐ **1.** Say, *Clap your hands if these words rhyme:*

  shoe, do **blue, blow** **few, do**
- ☐ **2.** Say, *Listen while I stretch these words. Tell me what the word is:*

  mm...an...y (many)
  s...ehn...t (sent)
  s...om...m (some)
- ☐ **3.** Say, *Now you try it. Stretch these words:* shoe, she.

Beginning to Read

- ☐ **1.** Ask your child to draw the poem and to tell you about the picture.
- ☐ **2.** Ask your child to circle words that name living things. Ask your child to make squares around words that are things but not alive.
- ☐ **3.** Say, *Let's play "What's the word?" We'll start with* old. *Now put a "g" sound at the beginning. What's the word?* (gold) *Now change the beginning sound to "t." What's the word?* (told) Repeat with "f" and "h."
- ☐ **4.** Write *sent* on a sheet of paper. Point out the *-ent* word family. Together, brainstorm, write, and read other words that rhyme and belong to the word family. (*bent, cent, dent, lent, rent, tent, went*) Help your child remember the spellings for the various words you make.
- ☐ **5.** Together, choose two or three words from the poem. Add them to your word wall and practice these words daily. Or add them to your child's word bank (a collection of words on cards, one word per card).

Hey Diddle Diddle

Hey diddle diddle,
The cat and the fiddle,
The cow jumped over
the moon.
The little dog laughed
To see such fun,
And the dish ran away
with the spoon.

Hey Diddle Diddle

Looking at Words and Letters

☐ **1.** Ask your child to count the words in the last line of the poem and to circle each word.

☐ **2.** Ask your child to find and underline all the *d*'s in the poem.

☐ **3.** Say, *This is the word* cow. *What letter does it start with?* Repeat with *cat, dish,* and *spoon.*

Playing With Sounds

☐ **1.** Say, *Clap your hands if these words rhyme:*

diddle, fiddle **cat, cow** **moon, spoon**

☐ **2.** Say, *Here are some riddles. The answers all rhyme with* fun.
I am in the sky. (sun)
I am what you put a hamburger in. (bun)
I mean "to move very quickly." (run)

☐ **3.** Say, *Raise your hand if these words end with the same sound:*

moon, ran **ran, fun** **cat, little**

Beginning to Read

☐ **1.** Ask your child to underline words that name living things.

☐ **2.** Ask your child to find words that name things that are not living and circle them.

☐ **3.** Put these words on index cards or little slips of paper. Then ask your child to sort them into two groups: words with one syllable (or beat) and words with two syllables (or beats). Words: *cat* (1), *fiddle* (2), *cow* (1), *moon* (1), *over* (2), *little* (2), *dog* (1), *laughed* (1), *dish* (1), *spoon* (1)

☐ **4.** Write *spoon* on a sheet of paper. Point out the *-oon* word family. Together, brainstorm, write, and read other words that rhyme and belong to the word family. (*moon, noon, soon*)

☐ **5.** Together, choose two or three words from the poem. Add them to your word wall and practice these words daily. Or add them to your child's word bank (a collection of words on cards, one word per card).

1, 2, 3, 4, 5

One, two, three, four, five,
Once I caught a fish alive.
Six, seven, eight, nine, ten,
Then I let it go again.
Why did you let it go?
Because it bit my finger so.
Which finger did it bite?
This little finger on the right!

1, 2, 3, 4, 5

Looking at Words and Letters

☐ **1.** Ask your child to underline words that start with "O."

☐ **2.** Ask your child to underline words twice that end with "o."

☐ **3.** Say, *Where is the first line in the poem? Circle the first word in the first line.* Repeat with the last line.

Playing With Sounds

☐ **1.** Ask your child to circle the number words and to write the numerals they go with.

☐ **2.** Say, *Guess the answers to these riddles. Everything will rhyme with* bite: *I am the opposite of wrong.* (right) *This is the opposite of loose.* (tight) *This is the opposite of day.* (night)

☐ **3.** Say, *Listen while I stretch these words:*
f...ou...r (four)
s...ii...x (six)
Now you try to stretch these words: five, seven, nine.

Beginning to Read

☐ **1.** Make two copies each of the number words. Play Concentration together.

☐ **2.** Ask your child to make a little picture of the poem and then tell you about the picture. Write down what he or she says, then read it together.

☐ **3.** Say, *Circle two words that rhyme and say them. Write two more words that also rhyme with the two you circled.*

☐ **4.** Write *five* on a sheet of paper. Point out the *-ive* word family. Together, brainstorm, write, and read other words that rhyme and belong to the word family. (*alive, arrive, dive, drive, hive*)

☐ **5.** Together, choose two or three words from the poem. Add them to your word wall and practice these words daily. Or add them to your child's word bank (a collection of words on cards, one word per card).

Flu

I'm wheezing
I'm sneezing
I'm coughing so loud.

I'm sputtering
I'm muttering
My head's in a cloud.

They say it's a fever,
They say it's the flu,
They say it's mysterious.
I say, "Ah . . . ah . . . CHOO!"

—Terry Cooper

Flu

Looking at Words and Letters

☐ **1.** Show your child the word *I'm*. Say, *This word means "I am." Put a circle around the other* I'm's *in the poem.*

☐ **2.** Show your child the word *they*. Say, *Find other times* they *is used in the poem. Put squares around them.*

☐ **3.** Ask your child to find and underline the lines that have only two words.

Playing With Sounds

☐ **1.** Say, *I will stretch out some words. You tell me what the words are:*
cl...ou...d (cloud)
f...l...u (flu)
mmm...utt...er...ing (muttering)

☐ **2.** Say, *Now you try it. Stretch out these words:* fever, sneezing.

☐ **3.** Ask your child how many syllables (beats) are in these words: *loud* (1), *coughing* (2), *mysterious* (4), *sputtering* (3).

☐ **4.** Say, *We'll start with the word* flu. *Change the first sound to "b." What's the word? Now change the first sound to "g." What's the word? Now change the first sound to "k." What's the word?*

Beginning to Read

☐ **1.** Ask your child to circle the words that end in *-ing* and to say the words without the *-ing*.

☐ **2.** Say, *Underline words that have the "f" sound. Watch out for the tricky one!* (coughing)

☐ **3.** Write *zing* on a sheet of paper. Point out the *-ing* word family. Together, brainstorm, write, and read other words that rhyme and belong to the word family. (*bring, king, ring, sing, wing*) Help your child see other words in the poem that end with *-ing*.

☐ **4.** Together, choose two or three words from the poem. Add them to your word wall and practice these words daily. Or add them to your child's word bank (a collection of words on cards, one word per card).

Little Boy Blue

Little Boy Blue, come blow your horn.
The sheep's in the meadow,
The cow's in the corn.
Where is the boy
who looks after the sheep?
He's under a haystack, fast asleep.
Will you wake him? No, not I!
For if I do, he's sure to cry.

Little Boy Blue

20

Looking at Words and Letters

☐ **1.** Say, *Count the words in the first line of the poem. Put your finger on each word as you count it.*

☐ **2.** Ask your child to circle the two lines that begin with the same word.

☐ **3.** Ask your child to underline all the *h*'s in the poem.

Playing With Sounds

☐ **1.** Say, *Clap your hands if the words start the same:*

boy, blue **cow, corn** **looks, cow's** **will, wake**

☐ **2.** Say, *Stretch out these three words into their sounds*: blow, sheep, blue

☐ **3.** Say, *Now I'll stretch out some words into sounds. You tell me what these words are:*
f…as…t (fast)
w…ay…k (wake)
c…r…y (cry)

☐ **4.** Say, *I'll say a word, then you say another word that rhymes. I say, "Cry." You say* _____.
(pie, my, sky, and so on) Repeat with *boy, blue, horn, him, wake.*

Beginning to Read

☐ **1.** Say, *Circle the words that start with* h. *Which one is* horn? *How do you know? Which one is* haystack? *How do you know? Which one is* him? *How do you know?*

☐ **2.** Ask your child to underline the words that name places and circle the words that name things.

☐ **3.** Say, *Let's write the word* blow. *Now we'll take the "l" out. What is the new word?* (bow) *Now we'll change the first letter to "t." What's the word?* (tow) *Now we'll take the last letter off. What's the word?* (to) *Now we'll add two letters at the end to make a word that means something is all ripped up. What's the word?* (torn) *Now change the first letter. What did Little Boy Blue blow?* (horn)

☐ **4.** Write *blow* and *horn* on a sheet of paper. Point out the word families -*ow* and -*orn*. Together, brainstorm, write, and read other words that rhyme and belong to these word families.

☐ **5.** Together, choose two or three words from the poem. Add them to your word wall and practice these words daily. Or add them to your child's word bank (a collection of words on cards, one word per card).

Baa, Baa Black Sheep

Baa, baa, black sheep,
Have you any wool?
Yes, sir, yes, sir,
Three bags full:
One for the master
And one for the dame
And one for the little boy
Who lives down the lane.

Baa, Baa Black Sheep

Looking at Words and Letters

- [ ] **1.** Ask your child to circle the words that start with L.
- [ ] **2.** Say, *Clap your hands if the words start the same:*

  little, lane **wool, little** **wool, full** **baa, boy**

- [ ] **3.** Ask your child to find a line that has two of the same words. Repeat.

Playing With Sounds

- [ ] **1.** Say, *Change the first sound of* dame *to answer the riddles. I am something like baseball.* (game) *I mean "not wild."* (tame) *I mean "just alike."* (same)
- [ ] **2.** Ask your child to stretch these words out: *wool, dame, lane.*
- [ ] **3.** Say, *I'll say a word. You say one that rhymes. I say,* "dame." *You say* ________. Repeat with *sheep, three, one, boy.*

Beginning to Read

- [ ] **1.** Put these words on index cards or little slips of paper. Ask your child to group them by the sound that "a" makes in the words: *black, any, bags, master, dame, lane.*
- [ ] **2.** Ask your child to circle the words that have two syllables (beats). (*any, master, little*)
- [ ] **3.** Ask your child to underline the words that name living things.
- [ ] **4.** Write *boy* and *sheep* on a sheet of paper. Point out the word families *-oy* and *-eep.* Together, brainstorm, write, and read other words that rhyme and belong to these word families.
- [ ] **5.** Together, choose two or three words from the poem. Add them to your word wall and practice these words daily. Or add them to your child's word bank (a collection of words on cards, one word per card).

Old King Cole

Old King Cole was a merry old soul,
A merry old soul was he;
He called for his pipe,
And he called for his bowl,
And he called for his fiddlers three.

Old King Cole

Looking at Words and Letters

☐ **1.** Point to the word *old* in the title. Say, *Can you find the word* old *three more times in the poem?*

☐ **2.** Ask your child to find three lines in the poem that start with the same letter and to circle the word that starts each line.

☐ **3.** Point to the word *he* in line two. Say, *Underline the word* he *in other places in the poem.*

Playing With Sounds

☐ **1.** Say, *Clap your hands if these words rhyme:*

Cole, bowl **bowl, pipe** **he, three**

☐ **2.** Say, *I will stretch out some words. You tell me what the words are:*
p…eye…p (pipe)
b…ow…l (bowl)
thr…ee (three)

☐ **3.** Say, *Now you stretch some words:* merry, Cole, called.

Beginning to Read

☐ **1.** Say, *Write the word* old. *Now add a letter to make a word that is the opposite of* hot. (cold) *Now change the last letter to make the king's name.* (Cole)

☐ **2.** Say, *Figure out these riddles. The answers will rhyme with* old. *This is what we do with laundry.* (fold) *I am a color.* (gold) *Today I sell; yesterday I _____.* (sold) *Today I tell; yesterday I _____.*(told)

☐ **3.** Ask your child to find "o" words from this poem and the previous one. Put these words on index cards or little slips of paper. Then have your child sort the words into three categories: long "o," short "o," and other sound of "o."

☐ **4.** Write *old* and *king* on a sheet of paper. Point out the word families *-old* and *-ing*. Together, brainstorm, write, and read other words that rhyme and belong to these word families.

☐ **5.** Together, choose two or three words from the poem. Add them to your word wall and practice these words daily. Or add them to your child's word bank (a collection of words on cards, one per card).

Hot Cross Buns

Hot cross buns,
Hot cross buns,
One a penny, two a penny,
Hot cross buns.
If your daughters don't like them,
Give them to your sons.
One a penny, two a penny,
Hot cross buns.

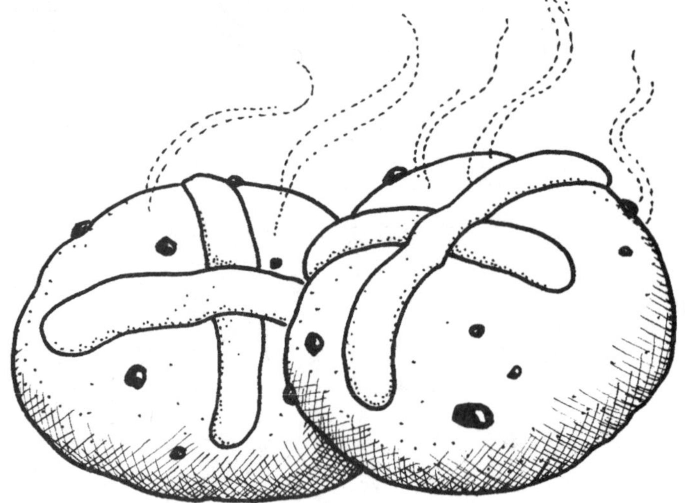

Hot Cross Buns

Looking at Words and Letters

- ☐ **1.** *Point to the word* buns *in the title. Say, Find this word in four other places in the poem.*
- ☐ **2.** Say *Find four lines in the poem that are the same and underline them.*
- ☐ **3.** Say *Circle all uppercase* H*'s and put boxes around the lowercase* h*'s.*
- ☐ **4.** Ask your child to count the words in the poem.
- ☐ **5.** Ask your child to point to the first and last word in the poem.

Playing With Sounds

- ☐ **1.** Say, *Let's play a rhyming game. I will say a word. You say one that rhymes. I say, "hot." You say* __________. Repeat with *cross, one, buns, like.*
- ☐ **2.** Say, *Let's think of words that rhyme with* hot. (List them as your child says them, offering clues if necessary.) *Now put as many as you can into a sentence. I'll write your sentence down for you.*
- ☐ **3.** Say, *I will stretch some words. You tell me what they are:*

  s…on…s (sons)
  p…en…ny (penny)
  g…iii…v (give)

  Now you try. Stretch these words: buns, hot, cross.

Beginning to Read

- ☐ **1.** Say, *What's the word? The answer will rhyme with* hot.

  I am a small mark. (dot)
  I am a pan for cooking. (pot)
  I am a little bed. (cot)

- ☐ **2.** Say, *Write* hot. *Now change the middle letter to make what happens with a ball and bat.* (hit) *Now change the middle letter again to make something you wear on your head.* (hat)
- ☐ **3.** Put all the words from above on index cards or little slips of paper. Make two cards or slips for each word. Use them to play Concentration or Go Fish.
- ☐ **4.** Write *bun* on a sheet of paper. Point out the *-un* word family. Together, brainstorm, write, and read other words that rhyme and belong to the word family (for instance, *fun, nun, pun, run, stun, sun*).
- ☐ **5.** Together, choose two or three words from the poem. Add them to your word wall and practice these words daily. Or add them to your child's word bank (a collection of words on cards, one word per card).

Little Jack Horner

Little Jack Horner
Sat in a corner,
Eating a Christmas pie.
He put in his thumb,
And pulled out a plum,
And said,
"What a good boy am I!"

Little Jack Horner

Looking at Words and Letters

- [ ] **1.** Say, *How many lines are in the poem? Number the lines.*
- [ ] **2.** Ask your child to look at the first line of the poem. Say, *Circle the first word. Now circle the last word.*
- [ ] **3.** Say, *Look at the last line in the poem. Circle each word.*

Playing With Sounds

- [ ] **1.** Ask your child to clap his or her hands if the words rhyme:

  thumb, plum **pie, plum** **I, pie**

- [ ] **2.** Say, *Guess the answer to these riddles. Each one will rhyme with* Jack.
  I am a small building. (shack)
  I am what you do with a suitcase. (pack)
  I am a pile of magazines all on top of each other. (stack)
- [ ] **3.** Say, *Stretch these words out into their sounds*: Jack, sat, thumb, said.

Beginning to Read

- [ ] **1.** Say, *Think of all the words you can that rhyme with* pie. *I'll write them down.* (Put *-ie* words in one list and *-y* words in another list.)
- [ ] **2.** Say, *Write the word* eat. *Change the first letter to make an animal.* (cat) *Now change the first letter to make a person's name—the short version of the name Patrick.* (Pat) *Now change the middle letter to make the seed inside a cherry.* (pit) *Now change the last letter to make what Little Jack Horner ate.* (pie)
- [ ] **3.** Write *plum* on a sheet of paper. Point out the *-um* word family. Together, brainstorm, write, and read other words that rhyme and belong to the word family. Help your child see the *-um* word family in *thumb*.
- [ ] **4.** Together, choose two or three words from the poem. Add them to your word wall and practice these words daily. Or add them to your child's word bank (a collection of words on cards, one word per card).

Winter Snow

What do you know!
It's beginning to snow.
You can hear the wind blow.
And the snowdrifts will grow.

What do you know!
The temperature is low.
Big snowballs we'll throw
In this winter white snow.

—Linda B. Ross

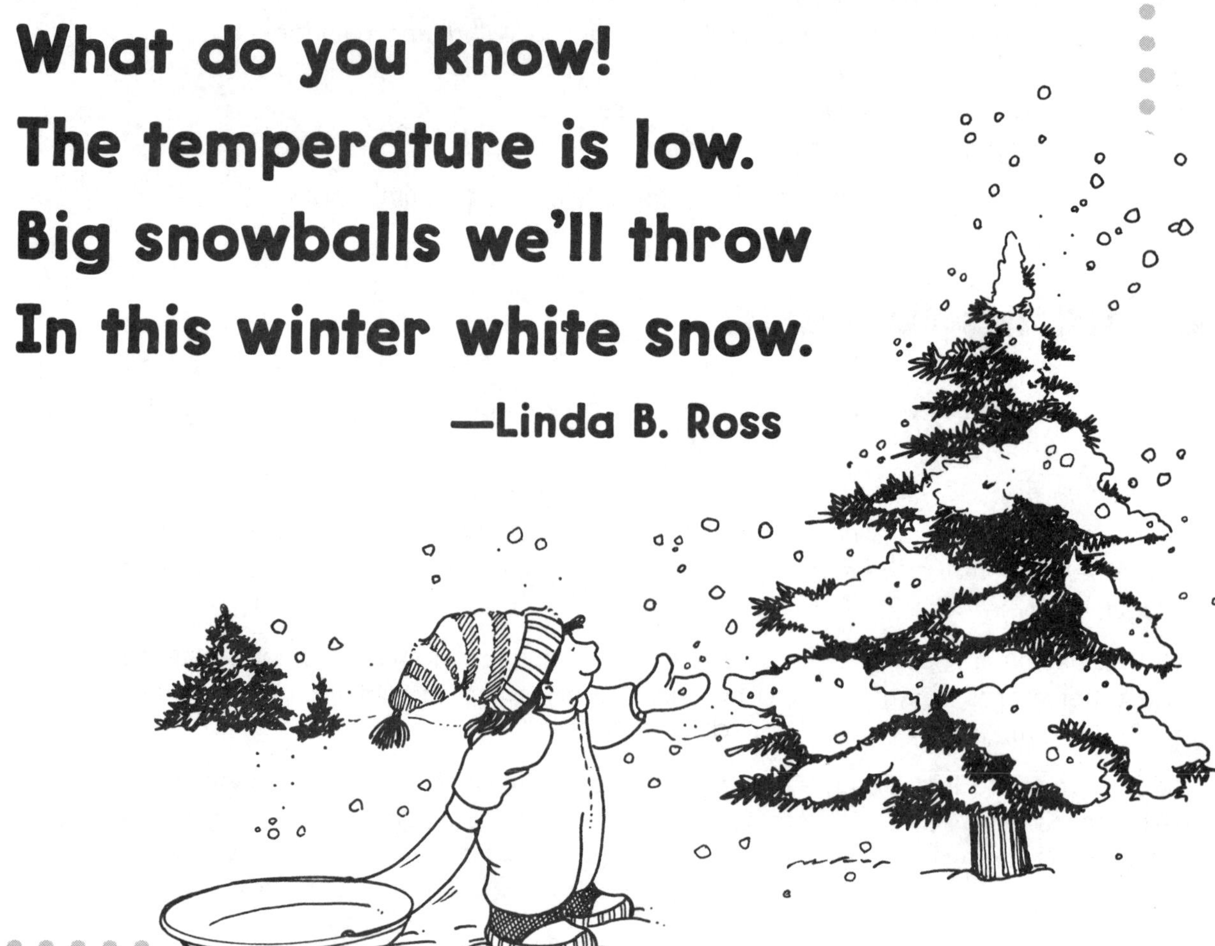

Winter Snow

Looking at Words and Letters

☐ **1.** Ask your child to find and circle all the *W*'s.

☐ **2.** Ask your child to find a line in the poem that begins and ends with a *W,w.* Repeat.

☐ **3.** Show your child the word *snow.* Say, *Find the word* snow *in other places in the poem.*

Playing With Sounds

☐ **1.** Say, *I will stretch some words that rhyme with* snow. *What's the word?*

l...oh...w (low)
n...oh...w (know)
bl...oh...w (blow)
gr...oh...w (grow)
th...roh...w (throw)

☐ **2.** Say, *Let's clap the poem.* (Do this once by yourself, then have your child join you.)

☐ **3.** Say, *Solve the riddles. Each one will rhyme with* snow. *I am the opposite of high.* (low) *Plants do this in the spring.* (grow) *I am the opposite of above.* (below)

Beginning to Read

☐ **1.** Ask your child to circle the one-syllable (or beat) words in the first stanza of the poem.

☐ **2.** Ask your child to put squares around the two-syllable (or beat) words in the second stanza of the poem.

☐ **3.** Play Concentration with *know, snow, low, grow, throw* (write each word on two slips of paper or index cards). Be sure to say the words as they are turned over.

☐ **4.** Write *snow* and *how* on a sheet of paper. Point out the *-ow* word family. Point out that the one word family represents two sounds. Together, brainstorm, write, and read other words that rhyme and belong to the two sounds of this word family (for instance *blow, know, low, row, show, snow;* and *cow, how, now*).

☐ **5.** Together, choose two or three words from the poem. Add them to your word wall and practice these words daily. Or add them to your child's word bank (a collection of words on cards, one word per card).

Twinkle, Twinkle

Twinkle, twinkle, little star,
How I wonder what you are.
Up above the world so high,
Like a diamond in the sky.

In the dark blue sky you keep,
Often through my curtains peep,
For you never shut your eye,
'Til the sun is in the sky.

Twinkle, twinkle, little star,
How I wonder what you are!

Twinkle, Twinkle

Looking at Words and Letters

☐ **1.** Show your child the word *Twinkle.* Say, *Find* twinkle *in other places in the poem.*

☐ **2.** Ask, *How many lines are in the poem?* Ask your child to number the lines.

☐ **3.** Ask your child to circle the words in line one. Repeat with line two.

Playing With Sounds

☐ **1.** Ask your child to find two words that rhyme in the poem. Repeat.

☐ **2.** Say, *I'll say one word. You say a word that rhymes. I say, "Star." You say _____.* Repeat with *how, like, sky, dark, sun.*

☐ **3.** Say, *Let's clap the poem.* (Do this once alone, if you need to.) *Now let's clap the first line. How many beats in* twinkle? little? star?

☐ **4.** Say, *I will stretch out some words into their sounds. You tell me the words:*

sk...y (sky)
sh...uh...t (shut)
st...a...r (star)

☐ **5.** Say, *Now you try stretching these words into sounds:* what, dark, blue.

Beginning to Read

☐ **1.** Say, High *and* sky *rhyme. Add more words that rhyme.* (Note: List words according to their spelling patterns.)

☐ **2.** Say, *Write the word* star. *Now drop the first letter. What's the word?* (tar) *Now change the first letter to "f." What's the word?* (far) *Now change the middle letter to make a word that means animal hair.* (fur) *Now change the last letter to make what we have at a party.* (fun) *Now change the first letter to make something else we see in the sky.* (sun)

☐ **3.** Say, *Solve the riddles. The answers will rhyme with* star. *I am the opposite of near.* (far) *You can drive me.* (car) *Jelly comes in me.* (jar)

☐ **4.** Write *star* and *keep* on a sheet of paper. Point out the *-ar* and *-eep* word families. Together, brainstorm, write, and read other words that rhyme and belong to these word families.

☐ **5.** Together, choose two or three words from the poem. Add them to your word wall and practice these words daily. Or add them to your child's word bank (a collection of words on cards, one word per card).

Bake a Cake

(sing to "Twinkle, Twinkle, Little Star")

If you want to bake a cake
It's not really hard to make

Take some sugar, eggs, and flour
Mix together, cook an hour

If you want to bake a cake
make it sweet for goodness sake!

—Teddy Slater

Bake a Cake

Looking at Words and Letters

- ☐ **1.** Ask your child to find and underline words that begin with "I."
- ☐ **2.** Ask your child to find and circle the words with "i" in the middle, and make a box around words that end in "e."
- ☐ **3.** Ask your child to find and draw squares around words that have two of the same letters right next to each other.

Playing With Sounds

- ☐ **1.** Put these words on index cards or little slips of paper: *cake, take, make, sake, bake.* Now say, *This is the word ____. Can you find it in the poem? Say the word.*
- ☐ **2.** Use the words above. Lay out all the cards so the words show. Say, *I will stretch these words. Tell me what each one is. Then find the word on the word cards.*
- ☐ **3.** Use the words once again. Say, *Now I will show you a word card. Stretch the word out.*

Beginning to Read

- ☐ **1.** Put these words on word cards: *cake, take, make, sake, bake*. Make two cards for each word. Then play Concentration or Go Fish together.
- ☐ **2.** Ask your child to circle the words in the poem that name things we could eat.
- ☐ **3.** Write *cake* on a sheet of paper. Point out the *-ake* word family. Together, brainstorm, write, and read other words that rhyme and belong to the word family.
- ☐ **4.** Together, choose two or three words from the poem. Add them to your word wall and practice these words daily. Or add them to your child's word bank (a collection of words on cards, one word per card).

Drip Drop

(sing to "Reuben, Reuben")

Drip drop, drip drop
on the rooftop
hear the rain fall:
plop plop plop
slip slop slip slop,
grab the mop-mop
won't that rainstorm ever stop?

—Teddy Slater

Drip Drop

Looking at Words and Letters

☐ **1.** Ask your child to find and put a check mark beside a line where all the words are the same.

☐ **2.** Ask your child to find and circle the words with "r" in them.

☐ **3.** Say, *Find and underline lines in the poem that have four words.*

Playing With Sounds

☐ **1.** Say, Drop *ends in this sound: "op." Can you think of other words that rhyme with* drop *and end in the* -op *sound?* Write them in one column for your child.

☐ **2.** Say, Drip *ends in this sound: "ip." Can you think of other words that rhyme with* drip *and end in the* -ip *sound?* Write them in another column for your child.

☐ **3.** Say, *Here are some new words. Where should we put them?* Depending on what your child offers above, you might want to use: *bop, hop, lop, mop, pop, sop, top, chop, shop; dip, hip, lip, pip, rip, sip, tip, blip, chip, ship, slip.*

Beginning to Read

☐ **1.** Say, *Here's the word* rip. *What word do we get if we add an* e *at the end?* (*ripe*) Repeat with *hop, mop, and pip.* (hope, mope, pipe)

☐ **2.** Make word cards for the words above. Play Concentration or Go Fish together. Match short-vowel words and long-vowel words (for instance, *rip* and *ripe*).

☐ **3.** Ask your child to use these word cards to make two groups: long vowel sounds and short vowel sounds.

☐ **4.** Write *drop* and *rope* on a sheet of paper. Point out the -*op* and -*ope* word families. Note in particular the short "o" and long "o" sounds. Together, brainstorm, write, and read other words that rhyme and belong to that word family.

☐ **5.** Together, choose two or three words from the poem. Add them to your word wall and practice these words daily. Or add them to your child's word bank (a collection of words on cards, one word per card).

The Crooked Man

There was a crooked man
And he walked a crooked mile.
He found a crooked sixpence
Against a crooked stile.
He bought a crooked cat,
Which caught a crooked mouse.
And they all lived together
In a crooked little house.

The Crooked Man

Looking at Words and Letters

- ☐ **1.** Ask your child to look at lines one and two. Which one has more words?
- ☐ **2.** Ask your child to circle each word in the last line of the poem.
- ☐ **3.** Say, *Find and underline words that contain the letter* c.

Playing With Sounds

- ☐ **1.** Say, *I will stretch out some words. You tell me what the word is*: man, mile, house. *Now you try. Stretch these words out*: stile, mouse.
- ☐ **2.** Say, *Fill in the blank with a word that rhymes with* stile:

  Let's jump into this _____ of leaves. (pile)
  Running a _____ would make me tired. (mile)
  What will you do _____ I cook dinner? (while)
- ☐ **3.** Say, *Clap your hands if these words end the same:*

  man, mile **mouse, house** **and, found** **little, mile**

Beginning to Read

- ☐ **1.** Ask your child to draw something in the poem and write a short sentence about it.
- ☐ **2.** Put the following words on slips of paper: *man, mile, sixpence, cat, mouse, house*. Then ask your child to sort the words: living things versus non-living things; words that start with the same sound versus words that don't start with the same sound; words that end with the same sound versus words that don't end with the same sound.
- ☐ **3.** Ask your child to find two words in the poem that rhyme. Then ask him or her to think of other words that rhyme with these two.
- ☐ **4.** Write *mile* on a sheet of paper. Point out the *-ile* word family. Together, brainstorm, write, and read other words that rhyme and belong to the word family.
- ☐ **5.** Together, choose two or three words from the poem. Add them to your word wall and practice these words daily. Or add them to your child's word bank (a collection of words on cards, one word per card).

Traveling, Traveling

(sing to "Row, Row, Row Your Boat")

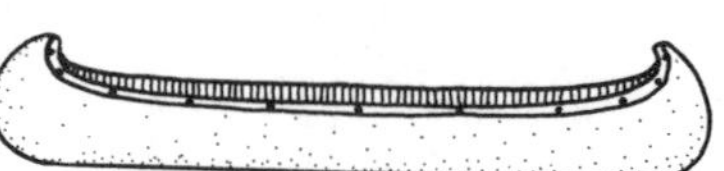

Row, row, row your boat,
Gently round the lake.
Traveling, traveling on the water,
Boats are what you take.

Drive, drive, drive your car,
Have a merry cruise.
Traveling, traveling on the road,
Cars are what you use.

Fly, fly, fly your plane,
High up in the air,
Traveling, traveling through the sky,
Planes will get you there.

Stamp, stamp, stamp your feet,
Stamp them on the ground.
Traveling, traveling on your feet,
Walk to get around!

—Meish Goldish

Traveling, Traveling

Looking at Words and Letters

☐ **1.** Sing stanza one together. Point to the words as you sing.

☐ **2.** Ask your child to find and circle three words that are the same in the first stanza. Repeat for other stanzas.

☐ **3.** Say, *This is the word* your. *Find it in other places in the poem. Put a square around the word* your *when you find it.*

☐ **4.** Ask your child to point to the first word in the poem and then to the last word in the poem.

Playing With Sounds

☐ **1.** Say, *Let's clap the syllables or beats in the first two stanzas.* You may want to do the first stanza alone and then invite your child to repeat it with you.

☐ **2.** Say, *Fill in the blanks with a word that rhymes with* take.

I want a chocolate _____ for my birthday. (cake)
If you blend ice cream and milk together, you can make a milk _____. (shake)
I usually _____ up at 7:00 in the morning. (wake)

☐ **3.** Say, *I will stretch out some words that rhyme with* air. *See if you can figure out what they are:*

b...ai...r (bear) *f...ai...r* (fair) *ch...ai...r* (chair)
th...ai...r (there) *p...ai...r* (pair)

Say, *Now you stretch out these words:* stamp, feet, get.

Beginning to Read

☐ **1.** Ask your child to circle all the words with long vowel sounds in the first stanza of the poem.

☐ **2.** Put these words on index cards or little slips of paper: *travel, traveling, drive, driving, row, rowing, stamp, stamping*. Play Concentration or Go Fish with the words. A pair would include both forms of the word (for instance, *row* and *rowing*).

☐ **3.** Say, *Write the word* row. *Now change the middle letter to make a word that means not cooked. What's the word?* (raw) *Now change the first letter to make a sound that crows make. What's the word?* (caw) *Now change the last letter to make an animal. What's the word?* (cat) *Now add a letter in the middle to make what we wear when it's cold outside. What's the word?* (coat) *Now change the first letter to make something we row.* (boat)

☐ **4.** Write *ground* on a sheet of paper. Point out the *-ound* word family. Together, brainstorm, write, and read other words that rhyme and belong to the word family.

☐ **5.** Together, choose two or three words from the poem. Add them to your word wall and practice these words daily. Or add them to your child's word bank (a collection of words on cards, one word per card).

Days of the Week

(sing to "Rock-a-Bye Baby")

Busy on Monday,
Reading a book.
Busy on Tuesday,
Helping to cook.
Busy on Wednesday,
Letters to write.
Busy on Thursday,
Flying my kite.
Busy on Friday,
Riding my bike.
Busy on Saturday,
Taking a hike.
Busy on Sunday,
Singing a song.
I am so busy
All the week long!

—Meish Goldish

Days of the Week

Looking at Words and Letters

- ☐ **1.** Ask your child to circle all the uppercase letters in the first four lines.
- ☐ **2.** Show your child the word *on*. Say, *Find* on *in other lines in the poem.*
- ☐ **3.** Say, *I will stretch out days of the week. You tell me which day I'm stretching.*
  M…un…day (Monday)
  S…un…day (Sunday)
  Wuh…ens…day (Wednesday)
  Th…urs…day (Thursday)
- ☐ **4.** Ask your child to count the words in the poem. Have your child point to where the poem begins and then to where it ends.

Playing With Sounds

- ☐ **1.** Ask your child to circle the days of the week.
- ☐ **2.** Say, *I will say and write a sound. You tell me two words from the poem that have the sound.* Say and write these for your child: *-ook, -ite, -ike, -ong.* Write your child's responses.
- ☐ **3.** Say, *now let's add more words that have these sounds.* Write them for your child.

Beginning to Read

- ☐ **1.** Write the days of the week on index cards or small slips of paper. Make two slips for each day. Play Concentration or Go Fish with them.
- ☐ **2.** Say, *Write the word* take. *Now change the first letter to make what the oven does. What's the word?* (bake) *Now change the second letter to make something we can ride. What's the word?* (bike) *Now change the first letter to finish this line: Busy on Saturday taking a* _____. (hike)
- ☐ **3.** Write *kite, bike,* and *song* on a sheet of paper. Point out the word families *-ite, -ike,* and *-ong.* Together, brainstorm, write, and read other words that rhyme and belong to the word families.
- ☐ **4.** Together, choose two or three words from the poem. Add them to your word wall and practice these words daily. Or add them to your child's word bank (a collection of words on cards, one word per card).

Winter Night

Winter winds are blowing,
Snow is drifting deep;
Cuddled under cover,
Earth has gone to sleep.

Cozy in their houses
Little children stay,
Where bright fires are burning
To keep the cold away.

Snug in caves and burrows
Wild things safe are curled,
While the feet of winter
Tramp across the world.

—Claude Weiner

Winter Night

32

Looking at Words and Letters

☐ **1.** Ask your child how many words are in the first line of the poem. Then ask how many words are in the last line of the poem.

☐ **2.** Ask your child to find and circle the words that begin with uppercase *W*.

☐ **3.** Ask your child to find and make boxes around all the lowercase *c's*.

Playing With Sounds

☐ **1.** Say, *I will say a sound. You tell me two words from the poem that have the sound.* Write these for your child: *-eep, -ay.*

☐ **2.** Say, *Now let's add more words that have these sounds.* Write them for your child.

☐ **3.** Say, *I will stretch the -eep words. You tell me which one I am saying:*

d...eee...p (deep)
sl...eee...p (sleep)
sh...eee...p (sheep)
p...eee...p (peep)

Beginning to Read

☐ **1.** Ask your child to illustrate the poem and tell you about the picture. Write down what your child says and read it together.

☐ **2.** Ask your child to circle all the "cold" words in the poem and underline all the "hot" words in the poem.

☐ **3.** Say, *I will say a letter of the alphabet. You tell me two words from the poem that start with that letter. One word should have one syllable (or beat), and one word should have two syllables (or beats).* Use W, D, B, C.

☐ **4.** Write *keep* and *stay* on a sheet of paper. Point out the *-eep* and *-ay* word families. Together, brainstorm, write, and read other words that rhyme and belong to the word families.

☐ **5.** Together, choose two or three words from the poem. Add them to your word wall and practice these words daily. Or add them to your child's word bank (a collection of words on cards, one word per card).

Sheep in a Jeep

(sing to "Farmer in the Dell")

Two sheep fell fast asleep,
Two sheep fell fast asleep,
Dreaming of two chickens,
riding in a jeep.
The jeep went beep-beep.
The chicks went peep-peep.
But both stayed quiet
In their deep, dreamy sleep.

—Teddy Slater

Sheep in a Jeep

Looking at Words and Letters

☐ **1.** Ask your child to count and number the lines in the poem.

☐ **2.** Ask your child to find and circle words that have two of the same letters together. Then say, *Now tell me the names of the letters.*

☐ **3.** Ask your child to find and draw boxes around the uppercase T's in the poem.

☐ **4.** Ask your child to find and underline two words that begin with "b" and underline them. Then ask your child to find two words that end with "p" and underline them twice.

Playing With Sounds

☐ **1.** Ask your child to find all the words in the poem that rhyme with *sheep*. Write them for your child.

☐ **2.** Say, *I will stretch these words. You tell me what word I'm stretching:*

sh…eee…p (sheep) *ah…sleee…p* (asleep) *j…eee…p* (jeep)
b…eee…p (beep) *p…eee…p* (peep) *sl…eee…p* (sleep)

☐ **3.** Say, *This time I will just say the first sound. You say the -eep word:* "sh," "j," "b," "p," "sl."

Beginning to Read

☐ **1.** Put these words on slips of paper: *sheep, fell, fast, asleep, dreaming, chicks, riding, went, stayed.* Ask your child to sort them into two piles: words with long vowels and words with short vowels.

☐ **2.** Using the same word cards, ask your child to sort them into words with one syllable (or beat) and words with two syllables (or beats).

☐ **3.** Say, *Write the word* sheep. *Now change the middle to a long "a" sound. What's the word?* (shape) *Now start this new word with a "t" sound. What's the word?* (tape) *Now end this new word with a "k" sound. What's the word?* (take)

☐ **4.** Write *fell* and *peep* on a sheet of paper. Point out the *-ell* and *-eep* word families. Together, brainstorm, write, and read other words that rhyme and belong to the word families.

☐ **5.** Together, choose two or three words from the poem. Add them to your word wall and practice these words daily. Or add them to your child's word bank (a collection of words on cards, one word per card).

Bill and Jill

(sing to "Mary Had a Little Lamb")

Bill went skiing down the hill,
took a spill, caught a chill.
Bill says he won't ski again.
There's no way that he will.
Jill went skiing down the hill,
fast and free, what a thrill.
Jill says she won't ever stop—
not until she's had her fill!

—Teddy Slater

Bill and Jill

Looking at Words and Letters

☐ **1.** Ask your child to put a check mark by the first and last lines of the poem.

☐ **2.** Ask your child to circle each word in the first and last lines of the poem.

☐ **3.** Say, *Find lowercase* i *in the first and last lines of the poem. How many lowercase* i's *did you find?* (six)

Playing With Sounds

☐ **1.** Ask your child to find all the words in the poem that have this sound: "ill".

☐ **2.** Say, *I will stretch some of these words. You tell me what the word is:*

h...ih...ll, (hill)
ch...ih...ll (chill)
w...ih...ll (will)
thr...ih...ll (thrill)

☐ **3.** Say, *Now you stretch some. See if you can trick me.*

Beginning to Read

☐ **1.** Ask your child to circle all the words in the poem that rhyme with *Jill.*

☐ **2.** Put the words on slips of paper. Make two copies of each word. Play Concentration or Go Fish with them.

☐ **3.** Say, *I will say some of these* -ill *words. You tell me what the word would be if it had a short "a" instead:* hill, Bill, will, till, fill.

☐ **4.** Write *hill* on a sheet of paper. Point out the *-ill* word family. Together, brainstorm, write, and read other words that rhyme and belong to the word family.

☐ **5.** Together, choose two or three words from the poem. Add them to your word wall and practice these words daily. Or add them to your child's word bank (a collection of words on cards, one word per card).

First Book

Hey everybody,
Come look, come look,

I'm reading, I'm reading,
I'm reading a book!

I just found it right here
On the library shelf
And I can read every word
All by myself.

Hey everybody,
Come look, come look!

I'm reading,
I'm reading,
My very first book!

—Linda Kulp

First Book

Looking at Words and Letters

☐ **1.** Ask your child to find two stanzas that are the same and to put a square around them.

☐ **2.** Say, *How many words in these stanzas are the same?*

☐ **3.** Show your child the word *reading*. Say, *Can you find and circle this word in other parts of the poem?*

☐ **4.** Ask your child to find a short word from the poem and write it down. Then ask your child to find a long word from the poem and write it down.

Playing With Sounds

☐ **1.** Say, *I will say a word. You say one that rhymes. I say, "Come." You say* _____. Repeat with *look, right, here, word, all.*

☐ **2.** Say, *Let's clap the syllables for the first two stanzas.* You may want to do this alone first. Then invite your child to join you.

☐ **3.** Say, *Here are some riddles. The answers rhyme with* book. *I am what you do on the stove.* (cook) *I am what goes on the end of fishing line.* (hook) *I am what the branches did when the wind blew.* (shook)

☐ **4.** Say, *Stretch these words from the poem into their sounds:*
shelf (sh…el…ff) *first* (f…irs…t) *book* (b…oo…k)

Beginning to Read

☐ **1.** Ask your child to draw a picture of the poem and then write a short description about it.

☐ **2.** Ask your child to circle the words in the poem that have something to do with reading.

☐ **3.** Say, *Write the word* read. *Change the first letter to make what's on top of our bodies. What's the word?* (head) *Now change the last letter to mean hot. What's the word?* (heat) *Now change the first letter to make what we do to a drum. What's the word?* (beat) *Now change the last letter to make a bird's nose. What's the word?* (beak) *Now change the middle two letters to make something we can read. What's the word?* (book)

☐ **4.** Write *book* on a sheet of paper. Point out the *-ook* word family. Together, brainstorm, write, and read other words that rhyme and belong to the word family.

☐ **5.** With your child, choose two or three words from the poem. Add them to your word wall and practice these words daily. Or add them to your child's word bank (a collection of words on cards, one word per card).

City Music

Snap your fingers.
Tap your feet.
Step out a rhythm
Down the street.

Rap on a litter bin.
Stamp on the ground.
City music
Is all around.

Beep says motorcar.
Ding says bike.
City music
Is what we like.

—Tony Mitton

City Music

Looking at Words and Letters

☐ **1.** Ask your child to find and underline three words that have three letters.

☐ **2.** Ask your child to find and draw circles around four words that have four letters.

☐ **3.** Say, *Look at the first four lines. Which word is longer in each line, the first or the last?*

Playing With Sounds

☐ **1.** Say, *Let's tap our feet to the syllables (or beats) in the poem.*

☐ **2.** Say, *I will say a word. You say another word that rhymes. I say, "snap." You say* _____. Repeat with *feet, step, all, bike, we.*

☐ **3.** Say, *Can you answer these riddles? Each one will rhyme with* street. *You walk on me.* (feet) *You do this on a drum.* (beat) *I am a special little surprise.* (treat)

Beginning to Read

☐ **1.** Ask your child to circle all the words that have something to do with noise.

☐ **2.** Say, *Look at the first stanza. Draw a box around words that have short vowel sounds. Underline the words that have long vowel sounds.*

☐ **3.** Put these words on slips of paper: *car, bike, fingers, feet, street, bin, ground.* Ask your child to sort the words into categories: "outside" word, "inside" word, or both; long vowel, short vowel, or neither; part of a living thing or not part of a living thing.

☐ **4.** Write *feet* and *bike* on a sheet of paper. Point out the word families *-eet* and *-ike.* Together, brainstorm, write, and read other words that rhyme and belong to the word families.

☐ **5.** Together, choose two or three words from the poem. Add them to your word wall and practice these words daily. Or add them to your child's word bank (a collection of words on cards, one word per card).

My Nose

It doesn't breathe;
It doesn't smell;
It doesn't feel
So very well.

I am discouraged
With my nose:
The only thing
It does is blows.

—Dorothy Aldis

My Nose

Looking at Words and Letters

☐ **1.** Ask your child to count and number the lines in the poem.

☐ **2.** Say, *Look at the two stanzas. Which one has only lines with three words?*

☐ **3.** Ask your child to circle the uppercase *I*'s and to underline the lowercase *i*'s.

Playing With Sounds

☐ **1.** Say, *Clap your hands if these words end the same:*

only, very **smell, feel** **nose, blows** **well, thing**

☐ **2.** Say, *I will say a word. You stretch it out:*
smell (sm…eh…ll)
feel (f…eee…l)
thing (th…in…g)
well (w…eh…ll)

☐ **3.** Say, *I will say a word. You tell me how many syllables (or beats) it has:* it, doesn't, smell, very, discouraged, nose

Beginning to Read

☐ **1.** Say, *Let's make a list of words that rhyme with* well.

☐ **2.** Put each of the words on a slip of paper. Make two slips for each word. Then play Go Fish or Concentration with them.

☐ **3.** Write *nose* on a sheet of paper. Point out the *-ose* word family. Together, brainstorm, write, and read other words that rhyme and belong to the word family. (*hose, pose, rose, chose, close, those*)

☐ **4.** Together, choose two or three words from the poem. Add them to your word wall and practice these words daily. Or add them to your child's word bank (a collection of words on cards, one word per card).

A Song of Sixpence

Sing a song of sixpence,
A pocket full of rye;
Four and twenty blackbirds
Baked in a pie.

When the pie was opened,
The birds began to sing;
Wasn't that a dainty dish
To set before the king?

A Song of Sixpence

Looking at Words and Letters

- ☐ **1.** Ask your child to find two lines with four words.
- ☐ **2.** Ask your child to find five lines with five words.
- ☐ **3.** Say, *circle uppercase* T's *and draw boxes around lowercase* t's.

Playing With Sounds

- ☐ **1.** Say, *Find three number words. Circle them. Write the numeral for each one.*
- ☐ **2.** Say, *Clap your hands if these words start the same.*

  sing, song **baked, began** **king, sing** **dainty, dish**
- ☐ **3.** Say, *I'll say a word. You say one that rhymes. I say, "sing." You say* _____. Repeat with *rye, set, dish, when.*

Beginning to Read

- ☐ **1.** Say, *I will say some words. You raise your hand if they have long vowel sounds:* sing, rye, blackbirds, pie, baked, dish, began.
- ☐ **2.** Put the following words on slips of paper: *pocket, rye, blackbirds, pie, birds, dish, king*. Ask your child to sort the words: one syllable or two syllables; living things or not living things.
- ☐ **3.** Ask your child to tell one thing in the poem that could not be true. Then ask for one thing in the poem that could be true. Ask "Why?" both times.
- ☐ **4.** Write *pie* and *sing* on a sheet of paper. Point out the word families *-ie* and *-ing*. Together, brainstorm, write, and read other words that rhyme and belong to the word families. (*die, tie, lie; bring, fling, wing*)
- ☐ **5.** Together, choose two or three words from the poem. Add them to your word wall and practice these words daily. Or add them to your child's word bank (a collection of words on cards, one word per card).

May on the Bay

(sing to "My Bonnie Lies Over the Ocean")

One day May went down to the seashore.
One day May went down to the bay.
She hopped in her little gray sailboat.
And then she went sailing away.
Away! Away! They say May
Went sailing away, away.
Away! Away!
Perhaps she'll come back some fine day.

—Teddy Slater

May on the Bay

Looking at Words and Letters

☐ **1.** Ask your child to count and number the lines in the poem.

☐ **2.** Say, *Where is the shortest line? How many words does it have? How many different words does it have?*

☐ **3.** Ask your child to find two lines that begin with the same two words. Repeat.

☐ **4.** Ask your child to count words in the first line and the last line of this poem. Ask which line has more words.

Playing With Sounds

☐ **1.** Say, *I will say two words. You clap your hands if they rhyme:*

day, May **bay, sail** **boat, bay** **say, gray**

☐ **2.** Say, *I will stretch some words. You tell me what the word is:*

Mm...aaa...y (May) *b...aaa...y* (bay)
s...aaa...y (say) *gr...aaa...y* (gray)
aw...aaa...y (away)

☐ **3.** Say, *I will say a word. You say one that rhymes. I say, "May." You say* _____. Repeat with *one, went, then, say, back*

Beginning to Read

☐ **1.** Say, *Let's find all the words that rhyme with May in the poem.* Make a list. *Now let's add to the list. What other words could we make with the sounds?* "tr," "pl," "w," "p," "kl," "l"? Write and read the words.

☐ **2.** Say, *Sometimes the -ay sound is spelled "eigh." Guess the riddles. They will all have the -ay sound.* Write the answers for your child. *I am what a horse says.* (neigh) *I am a horse-pulled sled people can ride on in the snow.* (sleigh) *I am the number after 7.* (eight) *If you step on a scale, you will find out about me.* (weight)

☐ **3.** Make double word cards for some of the words above. Play Go Fish or Concentration together.

☐ **4.** Together, choose two or three words from the poem. Add them to your word wall and practice these words daily. Or add them to your child's word bank (a collection of words on cards, one word per card).

Rub-a-Dub Cubs

(sing to "Row, Row, Row Your Boat")

Rub, rub, rub-a-dub.
Two bears in the tub.
Mama and her baby cub,
singing, "Rub-a-dub!"

Scrub, scrub, scrub-a-dub.
Join the sudsy club.
Bring some soap and sing along:
"Scrub-a-dub-a-dub!"

—Teddy Slater

Rub-a-Dub Cubs

Looking at Words and Letters

☐ **1.** Ask your child to find a line that begins with the letter *T*. Ask what letter the line ends with.

☐ **2.** Ask how many words are in that line. Have your child draw circles around the words.

☐ **3.** Say, *This is the word* Mama. *What letter does it begin with? What letter does it end with?* Repeat with *her, baby, cub.*

Playing With Sounds

☐ **1.** Say, *Answer these riddles. The answers will rhyme with* rub. *I am a baby bear.* (cub) *I am a place to take a bath.* (tub) *I mean "to wash."* (scrub)

☐ **2.** Say, *Clap your hands if these words start the same:*

bears, baby **sudsy, soap** **tub, club** **some, sing**

☐ **3.** Say, *I will say a word. You tell me how many syllables (beats) it has:* bears, tub, Mama, singing, join, sudsy.

☐ **4.** Say, *I'll say two words. Tell me if they have the same ending sound:*

soap, dip **rub, bib** **two, ten**

Beginning to Read

☐ **1.** Together, make word cards for all the *S* words. Ask your child to put them into two piles: one-syllable (or beat) words and two-syllable (or beat) words.

☐ **2.** Use the word cards above. Ask your child to find the words with short "u" (scrub, sudsy). Ask your child to find a word with long "o" (soap). Ask your child to find two words with endings. (*singing, sudsy*) Say, *What are the words without the endings?*

☐ **3.** Say, *Let's think of words that rhyme with* sing. *Here are some beginning sounds. You make the words.* "r," "th," "br," "d," "fl." Write and read the words.

☐ **4.** Write *rub* on a sheet of paper. Point out the *-ub* word family. Together, brainstorm, write, and read other words that rhyme and belong to the word family.

☐ **5.** Together, choose two or three words from the poem. Add them to your word wall and practice these words daily. Or add them to your child's word bank (a collection of words on cards, one word per card).

Baby Chick

Peck, peck, peck
On the warm brown egg.
Out comes a neck.
Out comes a leg.

How does a chick
Who's not been about,
Discover the trick
Of how to get out?

—Aileen Fisher

Baby Chick

41

Looking at Words and Letters

- ☐ **1.** Ask your child how many words are in the first line of the poem. Then ask how many different words are in the first line of the poem.
- ☐ **2.** Say, *Find the third line in the poem. Now find the fourth line in the poem. Circle the words that are the same in these two lines.*
- ☐ **3.** Ask your child to count the uppercase O's in the poem.

Playing With Sounds

- ☐ **1.** Say, *Answer the riddles with a word that rhymes with* chick. *I am the opposite of thin.* (thick) *I am a block that can be used to build a house.* (brick) *Soccer players do this to a ball.* (kick)
- ☐ **2.** Say, *Let's tap out the syllables (beats) in the poem.*
- ☐ **3.** Say, *I will stretch out some words. You tell me what they are.*

  p...eh...k (peck) *n...eh...k* (neck)
  d...eh...k (deck) *tr...eh...k* (trek)
- ☐ **4.** Say, *Tell me if these pairs of words rhyme:*

  peck, pick **neck, peck** **leg, egg** **trick, sick**

Beginning to Read

- ☐ **1.** Make a two-column chart: *-eck* words and *-ick* words. Ask your child to find words from the poem to go into each column. Then ask him or her to add other possible words.
- ☐ **2.** Make double word cards for some of the words. Play Go Fish or Concentration with them.
- ☐ **3.** Say, *Write the word* peck. *Now change the vowel to make a word that means something you do to a suitcase. What's the word?* (pack) *Now change the beginning sound to make a word that means an old, falling-down building. What's the word?* (shack) *Now change the vowel to make a word that describes what you could get from electricity. What's the word?* (shock) *Now change the first letter to make a word that means really, really full. What's the word?* (chock) *Now change the vowel to name something that can peck.* (chick)
- ☐ **4.** Write *chick* and *peck* on a sheet of paper. Point out the word families *-ick* and *-eck*. Together, brainstorm, write, and read other words that rhyme and belong to the word families.
- ☐ **5.** Together, choose two or three words from the poem. Add them to your word wall and practice these words daily. Or add them to your child's word bank (a collection of words on cards, one word per card).

Conversation

Cackle, gobble, quack, and crow,
Neigh and bray and bleat and low,
Twitter, chirrup, cheep, and coo,
Bark and growl and purr and mew.

Humming, buzzing, hiss, and sting,
Hoot and cuckoo, caw and sing,
Squeal and grunt and snort and squawk;
Who said, "Only people talk"?

—Althea M. Bonner

Conversation

Looking at Words and Letters

☐ **1.** Ask your child how many words are in the first line of the poem. Then ask how many words are in the second line of the poem. Finally, ask which line has more words.

☐ **2.** Show your child the word *and*. Say, *Find and circle all the* and's.

☐ **3.** Ask your child to look in the second stanza and underline all the words that begin with "s."

Playing With Sounds

☐ **1.** Say, *Clap your hands if these words start the same:*

cuckoo, caw **humming, buzzing** **squeal, squawk** **cackle, coo**

☐ **2.** Say, *Raise your hand if these rhyme:*

neigh, bray **bark, purr** **coo, mew** **squawk, talk**

☐ **3.** Say, *Answer the riddles with words that rhyme with* bark. *You could take a dog for a walk here or just play in me.* (park) *I am the opposite of light.* (dark) *You can make me with a pencil.* (mark) *I am a big ocean animal.* (shark)

☐ **4.** Say, *Stretch out these words into their sounds:* growl, only, people.

Beginning to Read

☐ **1.** Say, *I will say the name of an animal. You give me the word from the poem that names the sound it makes:* duck, horse, pig, owl.

☐ **2.** Make a two-column chart: one syllable and two syllables. Ask your child to put the animal sounds in the appropriate columns.

☐ **3.** Say, *When we add* -ing, hum *turns into* humming, *and* buzz *turns into* buzzing. *What is the new word when we add* -ing *to these words? Neigh, bray, hoot, sing, snort, squawk.*

☐ **4.** Write *crow* and *sting* on a sheet of paper. Point out the *-ow* and *-ing* word families. Together, brainstorm, write, and read other words that rhyme and belong to the word families.

☐ **5.** Together, choose two or three words from the poem. Add them to your word wall and practice these words daily. Or add them to your child's word bank (a collection of words on cards, one word per card).

Good-by and Hello

Good-by, ice skates.
Good-by, sled.
Good-by, winter,
Spring's ahead!

Good-by, leggings.
Good-by, snow.
Good-by, winter.
Spring, hello!

Hello, crocus.
Hello, kite.
Good-by, winter.
Spring's in sight!

Hello, jump rope.
Hello, swing.
Good-by winter!
Hello, spring!

—Barbara Anthony

Good-by and Hello

Looking at Words and Letters

☐ **1.** Ask your child how many lines are in the poem.

☐ **2.** Show your child the word *good-by*. Say, *Find and draw boxes around all the* good-by's *in the poem.*

☐ **3.** Show your child the word *hello*. Say, *Find and circle all the* hello's *in the poem.*

Playing With Sounds

☐ **1.** Say, *Answer the riddles with words that rhyme with* spring. *Birds use me to fly.* (wing) *I can be around your finger.* (ring) *A bee can do this.* (sting) *This is what you do with a song.* (sing)

☐ **2.** Say, *Let's clap the beats as we read the poem.*

☐ **3.** Say, *Let's start with the word* kite. *What word would we have if we changed the first sound to "f," "b," "r," "m," "n"?*

Beginning to Read

☐ **1.** Make a two-column chart: Winter and Spring. Ask your child to find words from the poem that belong in one of the categories.

☐ **2.** Put the words from the chart on index cards or little slips of paper. Ask your child to put them into other groups that make sense, such as long vowel sounds and short vowel sounds, or one-syllable words and two-syllable words.

☐ **3.** Say, *Start with the word* spring. *Drop two letters to make what we do with a song.* (sing) *Change the first letter to make what birds use to fly.* (wing) *Change the last letter to make something you can do with your eye.* (wink)

☐ **4.** Write *sled* and *spring* on a sheet of paper. Point out the *-ed* and *-ing* word families. Together, brainstorm, write, and read other words that rhyme and belong to the word families.

☐ **5.** Together, choose two or three words from the poem. Add them to your word wall and practice these words daily. Or add them to your child's word bank (a collection of words on cards, one per card).

I Talk

Kittens mew,
Doves coo.

Birds cheep,
Chicks peep.

Lions growl,
Dogs howl.

Monkeys chatter,
Starlings clatter.

Ducks quack,
Hens clack.

Parakeets squawk,
But *I talk*.

—Magdalen Eichert

I Talk

Looking at Words and Letters

☐ **1.** Say, *Find the line in the poem that has three words. Underline the line. Draw lines between the words.*

☐ **2.** Say, *I will point to a word. You tell me what letter it starts with:* Kittens, Doves, Birds, Chicks, Lions, Dogs.

☐ **3.** Ask your child to find and circle the uppercase *C*'s and the lowercase *c*'s.

Playing With Sounds

☐ **1.** Say, *Answer the riddles with words that rhyme with* chatter. *I hold the bat and stand at the plate.* (batter) *I am a big dish for serving food.* (platter) *I am the opposite of skinnier.* (fatter) *I am a loud noise.* (clatter)

☐ **2.** Say, *Let's clap the beats as we read the poem.*

☐ **3.** Say, *Let's begin with* cheep. *What word would we have if the beginning sound was "h," "b," "d," "k," "p," "sh."*

☐ **4.** Say, *Stretch these words out into their sounds:*

cheep (ch…eee…p)	*growl* (gr…ow…ell)
clack (cl…aa…k)	*quack* (qu…aa…k)

Beginning to Read

☐ **1.** Say, *Write the word* dog. *Change the first sound to make another name for a pig.* (hog) *Now change the last letter to fit in this sentence: _____ much does the new toy cost?* (How) *Now add a letter to make a noise that dogs make.* (howl)

☐ **2.** Say, *I will say the animal. You tell me what sound it makes in the poem: kitten, dove, chick, lion, dog.*

☐ **3.** Ask your child to find two animal sounds with one syllable, and then two animal sounds with two syllables.

☐ **4.** Write *quack* and *cheep* on a sheet of paper. Point out the *-ack* and *-eep* word families. Together, brainstorm, write, and read other words that rhyme and belong to the word families.

☐ **5.** Together, choose two or three words from the poem. Add them to your word wall and practice these words daily. Or add them to your child's word bank (a collection of words on cards, one word per card).

Oh, What a Shame!

I got sick,
Oh, what a shame.
Now I can't play
In the soccer game.
There's nothing to do.
There's no one to blame.
But all the same,
Oh, what a shame!

—Linda B. Ross

Oh, What a Shame!

Looking at Words and Letters

☐ **1.** Ask your child to find and put check marks beside lines that have four words.

☐ **2.** Ask your child to find and circle uppercase *T*'s and lowercase *t*'s.

☐ **3.** Say, *I will show you some words. You tell me what letter they end with:* got, sick, what, shame.

Playing With Sounds

☐ **1.** Say, *Answer the riddles with words that rhyme with* shame. *Tomorrow I will come, but yesterday I ____.* (came) *I am the opposite of wild.* (tame) *I am the opposite of different.* (same) *I am the fire on the top of a candle.* (flame)

☐ **2.** Say, *I will stretch some words. You tell me what they are:*

sh...aaa...me (shame) *pl...aaa...y* (play)
g...aaa...me (game) *s...aaa...me* (same)
bl...aaa...me (blame)

☐ **3.** Say, *Clap your hands if these words start the same:*

sick, shame **sick, soccer** **soccer, there** **blame, same**

Beginning to Read

☐ **1.** Ask your child to draw the poem and to write a few words about it.

☐ **2.** Make a two-column chart: *-ay* and *-all*. Ask your child to find two words from the poem to go on the chart. Together, brainstorm other words to go on the chart.

☐ **3.** Write *sick* and *blame* on a sheet of paper. Point out the *-ick* and *-ame* word families. Together, brainstorm, write, and read other words that rhyme and belong to the word families.

☐ **4.** Together, choose two or three words from the poem. Add them to your word wall and practice these words daily. Or add them to your child's word bank (a collection of words on cards, one word per card).

46

That Marching Beat

(sing to "Old MacDonald")

Clap your hands and stamp your feet.
Hear that marching beat.
Snap your fingers. Tap your toes.
Get up from your seat.
Make your elbows flap.
Give your palms a slap.
Here a clap, there a flap,
everywhere a snap, snap.
Clap your hands and tap your feet.
Hear that marching beat.

—Teddy Slater

That Marching Beat

Looking at Words and Letters

- ☐ **1.** Ask your child to circle the first word and then the last word in the poem.
- ☐ **2.** Ask your child to count and number the lines in the poem.
- ☐ **3.** Say, *Pick a line in the poem. Draw a box around each word in that line.* Repeat.
- ☐ **4.** Say, *Here is the word* clap *in the poem. What letters are in* clap?

Playing With Sounds

- ☐ **1.** Say, *I will stretch these* -ap *words. You tell me what the word is:*

  cl...aaa...p (clap) *sn...aaa...p* (snap)
  t...aaa...p (tap) *fl...aaa...p* (flap)
  sl...aaa...p (slap)

- ☐ **2.** Say, *Now you try it. Stretch these words:* snap, flap, slap.
- ☐ **3.** Say, *I will say a word from the poem. You say another word that rhymes. I say, "feet." You say* _____. Repeat with *toes, flap, that, up.*

Beginning to Read

- ☐ **1.** Ask your child to find five words with short vowel sounds. (*clap, hands, stamp, that, snap, tap, get, up, flap, give, slap*) Then ask your child to find five words with long vowel sounds. (feet, hear, beat, toes, seat, make, here, there)
- ☐ **2.** Say, *I will say some words. You tell me how many syllables (or beats) they have:* clap, marching, snap, fingers, elbows, flap, everywhere.
- ☐ **3.** Say, *Circle all the words in the poem that are things you could do. Now do these things.*
- ☐ **4.** Write *feet, beat,* and *flap* on a sheet of paper. Point out the word families *-eet, -eat,* and *-ap.* Together, brainstorm, write, and read other words that rhyme and belong to the word families. Point out that *-eet* and *-eat* have the same sound but different spellings. Help your child remember words that are spelled with each word family.
- ☐ **5.** Together, choose two or three words from the poem. Add them to your word wall and practice these words daily. Or add them to your child's word bank (a collection of words on cards, one word one per card).

My New Red Bike

(sing to "Mulberry Bush")

**I'd like to ride my new red bike,
new red bike, new red bike.
I'd like to ride my new red bike
all around the town.**

**Mike and Ike would rather hike,
rather hike, rather hike,
Mike and Ike would rather hike,
and so would their dog, Spike.**

—Teddy Slater

My New Red Bike

Looking at Words and Letters

- [ ] **1.** Ask your child to count and circle the words in the first line of the poem.
- [ ] **2.** Ask your child to find words that begin with the letter *l*.
- [ ] **3.** Say, *Here is the word* like. *What letter does it begin with? What are the rest of the letters?* Repeat with *bike*, *Mike*, and *hike*.

Playing With Sounds

- [ ] **1.** Say, *Answer the riddles with a word that rhymes with* bike. *I am the nickname for a three-wheeled bike.* (trike) *I am the nickname for a microphone.* (mike) *Yesterday I liked, but today I* ______. (like)
- [ ] **2.** Say, *Raise your hand if the words end the same:*

ride, would **Spike, hike** **around, town** **new, so**

- [ ] **3.** Say, *I'll say a word. You say one that rhymes. I say, "ride." You say* _____. Repeat with *new, red, my, so*.

Beginning to Read

- [ ] **1.** Say, *Start with the word* ride. *Change the first letter to make a game,* _____ *and Seek.* (Hide) *Change the last sound to make a walk in the woods.* (hike) *Change the first letter to make something you can ride.* (bike)
- [ ] **2.** Say, *I will say a word with a long "i" sound. You tell me what the word would be with a short "i" sound: ride* (rid), *like* (lick), *trike* (trick), *Mike* (Mick), *pike* (pick).
- [ ] **3.** Say, *This time I will say a word with a long "i" sound and you say a word with a long "a" sound: Mike* (make), *bike* (bake), *ride* (raid).
- [ ] **4.** Write *hike* and *ride* on a sheet of paper. Point out the *-ike* and *-ide* word families. Together, brainstorm, write, and read other words that rhyme and belong to the word families.
- [ ] **5.** Together, choose two or three words from the poem. Add them to your word wall and practice these words daily. Or add them to your child's word bank (a collection of words on cards, one word per card).

The Shape of Things

What is a circle? What is round?
A quarter rolling on the ground.
A wheel is a circle, so is the moon,
A bottle cap, or a big balloon.

What is a square, with sides the same?
The wooden board for a checker game.
A slice of cheese, a TV screen,
A table napkin to keep you clean.

These are the shapes seen everywhere:
A triangle, rectangle, circle, square.
If you look closely where you've been,
You'll surely see the shapes again!

—Meish Goldish

The Shape of Things

Looking at Words and Letters

☐ **1.** Ask your child how many lines are in the first stanza of the poem. Then ask how many words are in the first stanza of the poem.

☐ **2.** Say, *Find five uppercase A's. Circle them. Now find five lowercase a's. Put boxes around them.*

☐ **3.** Show your child a question mark. Say, *Find other question marks in the poem. Now make your own question mark.*

Playing With Sounds

☐ **1.** Say, *I'll stretch some words. You tell me what they are:*
ss...aaa...me (same) *sh...aap...es* (shapes) *ss...eee...n* (seen)
squ...aa...re (square) *su...re...ly* (surely)

☐ **2.** Say, *Answer the riddles with words that rhyme with* wheel. *If you're sick, you don't _____ good.* (feel) *I am an animal that lives in the water or on land.* (seal) *You should _____ an orange before you eat it.* (peel) *Breakfast is a _____.* (meal)

☐ **3.** Go through the same words as above. Ask your child if the pairs rhyme.

Beginning to Read

☐ **1.** Ask your child to find ten words from the poem that have long vowel sounds. (rolling, wheel, so, square, sides, same, game, slice, cheese, screen, table, keep, clean, these, shapes, seen, everywhere, triangle, rectangle, closely, where, see)

☐ **2.** Put the following words on index cards or little slips of paper: *board, screen, napkin, quarter, wheel.* Ask your child to sort the words into two groups: round things or square things. Then invite your child to add other round and square things to the list.

☐ **3.** Using the same set of words, ask your child to sort as follows: long vowel sound or short vowel sound, and one-syllable words or two-syllable words.

☐ **4.** Write *round, game, clean,* and *screen* on a sheet of paper. Point out the word families *-ound, -ame, -ean,* and *-een.* Together, brainstorm, write, and read other words that rhyme and belong to the word families.

☐ **5.** Together, choose two or three words from the poem. Add them to your word wall and practice these words daily. Or add them to your child's word bank (a collection of words on cards, one word per card).

Away We Go

Hippity-hop!
Skippity-skop!
We've hopped so long
Our feet won't stop.

We say hello
To those we meet
And hippity-hop
On down the street.

—Eleanor Dennis

Away We Go

Looking at Words and Letters

☐ **1.** Ask your child to count and number the lines in the poem.

☐ **2.** Line by line, ask your child to point to the first word in each line and tell you what letter begins each word.

☐ **3.** Line by line, ask your child to point to the last word in each line of the poem and to tell you what letter ends each word.

Playing With Sounds

☐ **1.** Say, *Answer the riddle. The answer will rhyme with* hop. *I mean "to cut up into little pieces."* (chop) *If you do this to a glass, it will break.* (drop) *This is what you do in a store.* (shop)

☐ **2.** Say, *How many syllables (or beats) are in the first line of the poem?* (4) *The second line?* (4) *The third line?* (4) *The fourth line?* (4)

☐ **3.** Say, *I'll say a word. You say its opposite using a word from the poem. I say "short." You say* _____. Repeat with *go, good-bye, up.*

Beginning to Read

☐ **1.** Put the following words on index cards or small slips of paper: *hop, feet, hello, so, say, meet, and, on, street.* Ask your child to sort the words into two categories: long vowel sounds and short vowel sounds.

☐ **2.** Ask your child to find two words that rhyme and then to think of some more words that rhyme with these two.

☐ **3.** Say, *Write the word* hop. *Now change the middle letter to make a bone that connects your legs to your body.* (hip) *Now change the last letter to make something that would make a baseball player happy.* (hit) *Now change the middle sound to make the noise an owl makes.* (hoot) *Now change the first letter to make 12 inches.* (foot) *Now change the middle letters to make what hopped in the poem.* (feet)

☐ **4.** Write *hop* and *long* on a sheet of paper. Point out the *-op* and *-ong* word families. Together, brainstorm, write, and read other words that rhyme and belong to the word families.

☐ **5.** Together, choose two or three words from the poem. Add them to your word wall and practice these words daily. Or add them to your child's word bank (a collection of words on cards, one word per card).

Opposites

(sing to "Ten Little Indians")

You say yes, and I say no,
You say stop, and I say go,
You say fast, and I say slow,
These are opposites!

You say day, and I say night,
You say dark, and I say bright,
You say heavy, I say light,
These are opposites!

You say big, and I say small,
You say short, and I say tall,
You say none, and I say all,
These are opposites!

You say wet, and I say dry,
You say low, and I say high,
You say laugh, and I say cry,
These are opposites!

—Meish Goldish

Opposites

Looking at Words and Letters

☐ **1.** Ask your child to find three lines that start the same.

☐ **2.** Show your child the word *say*. Say, *Find and draw a square around the word in other places in the poem.*

☐ **3.** Show your child the word *you*. Say, *Find and circle the word* you *in other places in the poem.*

Playing With Sounds

☐ **1.** Say, *I will say a word from the poem. You say its opposite. I say, "yes." You say _____.* Repeat with *stop, slow, small, big.*

☐ **2.** Say, *Clap your hands if they start the same:*

day, dark **low, laugh** **stop, fast** **heavy, high**

☐ **3.** Say, *Let's start with the sound "oh." What word will we have if the beginning sound is "b," "bl," "fl," "m," "s," "sh"?*

☐ **4.** Say, *Here are some words. Tell me what new word you can make if the first sound is removed from each word:* bright, small, tall, stop.

Beginning to Read

☐ **1.** Say, *Find words that are opposites. You tell them to me, and I'll write them on index cards or little slips of paper.* Play Go Fish or Concentration with the opposites. (A match will be the word and its opposite.)

☐ **2.** Say, *I'll say some more words. You tell me the opposite*: up, under, in, early, morning.

☐ **3.** Write *night* and *small* on a sheet of paper. Point out the *-ight* and *-all* word families. Together, brainstorm, write, and read other words that rhyme and belong to the word families.

☐ **4.** With your child, choose two or three words from the poem. Add them to your word wall and practice these words daily. Or add them to your child's word bank (a collection of words on cards, one word per card).

Listen!

The rain

Hits the puddles
Pop-pop-plop

Pings the roof
Spat-a-tat-tat

Zaps the sidewalks
Sizzily-pizzily

Slaps the ground
Woppity-thud

Smoozily-oozily
Squooshes to mud.

—Jacqueline Sweeney

Listen!

Looking at Words and Letters

☐ **1.** Ask your child to count the words in the first line of the poem and then to count the words in the last line of the poem.

☐ **2.** Ask your child to find and underline the uppercase *S*'s and the lowercase *s*'s.

☐ **3.** Show your child the word *the*. Say, *Find and draw circles around the word* the *in other places in the poem.*

☐ **4.** Say, *Point to the first line in the poem. Point to the last line. Point to the first word in the poem. Point to the last word. Point to the first word in the last line of the poem.*

Playing With Sounds

☐ **1.** Say, *I will say a word from the poem. You say one that rhymes. I say, "ground." You say* _____. Repeat with *mud*, *slap*, and *ping*.

☐ **2.** Ask, *How many syllables (or beats) are in the last stanza of the poem? In the second to last stanza?*

☐ **3.** Say, *Answer these riddles with words that rhyme with* rain. *I go on tracks.* (train) *You think with me.* (brain) *I am another name for a necklace.* (chain) *If you* _____ *your ankle, you will be in* _____. (sprain, pain)

Beginning to Read

☐ **1.** Say, *Write the word* rain. *Now drop a letter to fill in this blank: Today I run, but yesterday I* _____. (ran) *Now change the first letter to make a grown up male.* (man) *Now change the last letter to make another word for angry.* (mad) *Now change the middle letter to make what becomes dirt when it rains.* (mud)

☐ **2.** Ask your child to illustrate this poem and then to write a sentence to describe it.

☐ **3.** Ask, *Which four words describe what the rain did? Think of a word that rhymes with each one.*

☐ **4.** Write *rain* and *mud* on a sheet of paper. Point out the *-ain* and *-ud* word families. Together, brainstorm, write, and read other words that rhyme and belong to the word families.

☐ **5.** Together, choose two or three words from the poem. Add them to your word wall and practice these words daily. Or add them to your child's word bank (a collection of words on cards, one word per card).

My Dog

His feet are big,
His ears are floppy.
When he eats
He's very sloppy.
He can't do tricks,
Jump over sticks
Or anything that's clever.
But he's my own,
My very own,
And I'll love him
Forever!

—Helen Lorraine

My Dog

Looking at Words and Letters

☐ **1.** Ask your child how many lines in the poem begin with capital *H.*

☐ **2.** Say, *How many words are in the first line of the poem? How many words are in the second line of the poem?*

☐ **3.** Ask, *Where is the shortest line in the poem? How many words are in this line?*

Playing With Sounds

☐ **1.** Say, *I'll stretch some words. You tell me what they are.*

fl...opp...y (floppy) *sl...opp...y* (sloppy)
tr...ick...s (tricks) *st...ick...s* (sticks)

☐ **2.** Ask your child to illustrate the poem and tell you about what he or she has drawn.

☐ **3.** Say, *Answer the riddles with a word that rhymes with* flop. *If you do this, a glass will break.* (drop) *You can use me to clean the floor.* (mop) *You do this at the grocery store.* (shop) *If you jump on one foot, you do this.* (hop)

☐ **4.** Ask, *What words will you make if you take the last sound off of the words* floppy, tricks, *and* own? (flop, trick, owe)

Beginning to Read

☐ **1.** Ask your child to illustrate the poem and tell you about what he or she has drawn.

☐ **2.** Put these words on little slips of paper: *he's, he is, can't, cannot, that's, that is, I'll, I will.* Play Go Fish or Concentration with the slips of paper. The object is to match a contraction with its longer form (for instance, *he's* with *he is*).

☐ **3.** Ask your child to find the words in the poem that end with *y* or *s* and to say each one without the ending.

☐ **4.** Write *clever* and *stick* on a sheet of paper. Point out the word families *-ever* and *-ick* to your child. Together, brainstorm, write, and read other words that rhyme and belong to the word families.

☐ **5.** Together, choose two or three words from the poem. Add them to your word wall and practice the words on the word wall daily. Or, add them to your child's word bank (a collection of words on cards, one word per card).

Circle of We

(sing to "Goodnight Irene")

You are you. I am me.
He is he and she is she.
All together, that makes we.
He is he and she is she.
All together that makes we.
It's the nicest way to be.
You and me. You and me.
Oh, how happy we'll be.
Let's join hands
You and me
In the circle
of "we."

—Teddy Slater

Circle of We

Looking at Words and Letters

☐ **1.** Ask your child to circle all the words in the poem that begin with the letter *A*.

☐ **2.** Show your child the word *me*. Say, *Find and underline the word* me *in other places in the poem.*

☐ **3.** Say, *Find a very short word that starts with* T. *Find a long word that starts with* T.

☐ **4.** Say, *Point to the last word in the first line of the poem. Point to the last word in the second line of the poem. Point to the first word in the last line of the poem.*

Playing With Sounds

☐ **1.** Ask, *How many syllables (beats) are there in the first line of the poem?* (six) *in the second line?* (seven)

☐ **2.** Say, *We'll start with* me. *What is the word if we change the beginning sounds to* "f," "fl," "fr," "s," "sh," "t," "tr"?

☐ **3.** Say, *Clap your hands if the words start the same:*

me, makes **how, happy** **we, way** **we'll, all**

☐ **4.** Ask your child to stretch out these words into their sounds: *makes, she, happy, hands.*

Beginning to Read

☐ **1.** Ask your child to circle all the words that refer to people and to put them on slips of paper.

☐ **2.** Say, *I will say some people. You tell me which word could mean the same thing.* (you, she, he, me, we) *Here's one to begin: My mother.* (she) My father. (he) My sister. (she) My brother. (he) Your teacher. (she or he) All of us. (we)

☐ **3.** Ask your child to find the words in the poem that have the long "e" vowel sound.

☐ **4.** Write *me* and *hand* on a sheet of paper. Point out the *-e* and *-and* word families. Together, brainstorm, write, and read other words that rhyme and belong to the word families.

☐ **5.** Together, choose two or three words from the poem. Add them to your word wall and practice these words daily. Or add them to your child's word bank (a collection of words on cards, one word per card).

One Magical Midnight

(sing to "On Top of Old Smokey")

One magical midnight,
the moon turned to gold,
an old man grew young and
a shy boy grew bold.
The North Pole got hot and
the South Seas got cold.
Such things sometimes happen . . .
or so I've been told.

—Teddy Slater

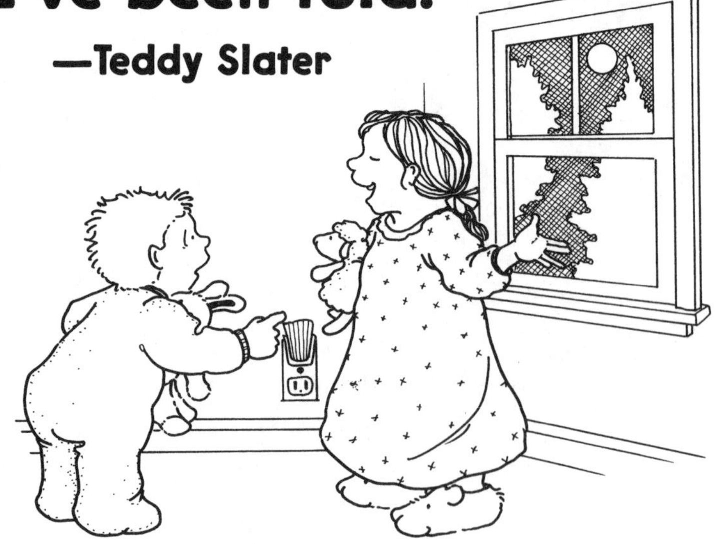

One Magical Midnight

★54★

Looking at Words and Letters

☐ **1.** Ask your child to count and number the lines in the poem.

☐ **2.** Say, *Circle each word in the first line of the poem. Now circle each word in the last line of the poem.*

☐ **3.** Ask your child to find and draw boxes around three words that begin with uppercase *S*.

Playing With Sounds

☐ **1.** Say, *Listen while I stretch out these* -old *words. You tell me what the word is:*

c...ol...d (cold)
b...ol...d (bold)
t...ol...d (told)
g...ol...d (gold)

☐ **2.** Say, *Now you try. Stretch out* bold, cold, gold, told.

☐ **3.** Say, *Raise your hand if these words start the same:*

boy, bold **south, such** **north, south** **cold, bold**

Beginning to Read

☐ **1.** Ask your child to find two compound words from the poem and to tell you the word parts for each one. (*midnight, sometimes*)

☐ **2.** Ask, *Do you think the story told in this poem could really be true? Why?*

☐ **3.** Write *gold* and *midnight* on a sheet of paper. Point out the word families -*old* and -*ight*. Together, brainstorm, write, and read other words that rhyme and belong to the word families.

☐ **4.** Together, choose two or three words from the poem. Add them to your word wall and practice these words daily. Or add them to your child's word bank (a collection of words on cards, one word per card).

Watering a Rose

(sing to "If You're Happy and You Know It")

If you're watering a rose,
turn on the hose.
If your picture's being taken,
strike a pose.
If a skunk is coming near,
hold your nose, then disappear.
'Cause it's no fun to get a whiff
of one of those.

—Teddy Slater

Watering a Rose

Looking at Words and Letters

- ☐ **1.** Say, *Point to the shortest line in the poem. How many words are in the shortest line?*
- ☐ **2.** Ask your child to count and draw lines between all the words in the first line of the poem.
- ☐ **3.** Ask your child to circle all the words with the letter *f*.

Playing With Sounds

- ☐ **1.** Say, *Clap your hands if these words rhyme:*

  rose, pose **near, nose** **skunk, trunk** **hose, hold**
- ☐ **2.** Ask your child to find five words in the poem that have one syllable and then to find three words that have two syllables.
- ☐ **3.** Say, *I'll say a word. You say one that rhymes. I say, "rose." You say* _____. Repeat with *turn, near, fun, those.*
- ☐ **4.** Say, *Let's change some words. You tell me what the new word is. We'll begin with* hose. *Add a* t *to the end. What's the word?* (host). *Now change the first sound to "r." What's the word?* (roast). *Now change the last sound to "r." What's the word?* (roar). *Now change the last sound to "z." What's the word?* (rose).

Beginning to Read

- ☐ **1.** Ask, *Which words in the poem have two syllables?* (picture, being, taken, coming)
- ☐ **2.** Ask, *What is the vowel sound (short or long) in the first syllable of each of the above words?* (short, long, long, short)
- ☐ **3.** Write *hose* and *disappear* on a sheet of paper. Point out the word families -*ose* and -*ear*. Together, brainstorm, write, and read other words that rhyme and belong to the word families.
- ☐ **4.** Together, choose two or three words from the poem. Add them to your word wall and practice these words daily. Or add them to your child's word bank (a collection of words on index cards, one word per card).
- ☐ **5.** Ask your child to find and circle these words: *picture, whiff, disappear, skunk.*

Best Deal in Town

I go to the library after school
And find myself a book that's cool.
There is no charge,
The books are free.
Just how much better could it be?

—Betsy Franco

Best Deal in Town

Looking at Words and Letters

☐ **1.** Ask your child to count and number the lines in the poem.

☐ **2.** Say, *Count and circle each word in the first line of the poem.*

☐ **3.** Say, *Find a word that begins with* L *and two words that end with* l.

Playing With Sounds

☐ **1.** Say, *I'll say a word. You say one that rhymes. I say, "go." You say* _____. Repeat with *find, book, cool, free.*

☐ **2.** Ask, *How many syllables (beats) are there in the fourth line of the poem?* (4) *in the last line of the poem?* (8)

☐ **3.** Say, *We'll start with* cool. *What word would we have if we changed the beginning sound to "f," "p," "r," "t," "sk"?*

Beginning to Read

☐ **1.** Ask your child to illustrate the poem and write a sentence about it.

☐ **2.** Say, *Write the word* read. *Now drop a letter to make a color.* (red) *Now change the first letter to make a place for sleeping.* (bed) *Now change the middle letter to make the opposite of good.* (bad) *Now change the ending to make the opposite of front.* (back) *Now change the middle two letters to make something we can read.* (book)

☐ **3.** *Ask your child to find two words with two letters and long vowel sounds.* (go, no, be) *Then ask your child to find two words with four letters and long vowel sounds.* (find, free)

☐ **4.** Write *school, be,* and *free* on a sheet of paper. Point out the *-ool, -e,* and *-ee* word families. Together, brainstorm, write, and read other words that rhyme and belong to the word families. Help your child see that the -e and -ee word families make the same sounds. Help your child remember words that are spelled with each word family.

☐ **5.** Together, choose two or three words from the poem. Add them to your word wall and practice these words daily. Or add them to your child's word bank (a collection of words on cards, one word per card).

Jump or Jiggle

Frogs jump
Caterpillars hump

Worms wiggle
Bugs jiggle

Rabbits hop
Horses clop

Snakes slide
Seagulls glide

Mice creep
Deer leap

Puppies bounce
Kittens pounce

Lions stalk,
But
I walk!

—Evelyn Beyer

Jump or Jiggle

Looking at Words and Letters

☐ **1.** Say *I will point to some words in the poem. You tell me what letter they start with:* Mice, Deer, Snakes, Seagulls, Frogs.

☐ **2.** Ask your child to find and underline two words that end in *-op*.

☐ **3.** Ask your child to find and circle two words that end in *-alk*.

Playing With Sounds

☐ **1.** Say, *Clap your hands if the words start the same:*

puppies, pounce **hump, horses** **hop, clop** **walk, worms**

☐ **2.** Ask, *What is a grown up puppy called? Does it start with the same sound? What is a grown up kitten called? Does it start with the same sound? What is a baby horse called? Does it start with the same sound?*

☐ **3.** Say, *We'll start with* slide. *What if we changed the beginning sounds to* "d," "fr," "gl," "h," "l," "str"?

☐ **4.** Say, *Stretch out these words into their sounds:* slide, creep, pounce, stalk.

Beginning to Read

☐ **1.** Write the animal names on index cards or little slips of paper. Then ask your child to sort them: live outside, live inside, or both; have four legs or don't have four legs; can walk or cannot walk.

☐ **2.** Make a duplicate set of the animal cards. Play Go Fish or Concentration with them.

☐ **3.** Ask your child to sort the animal words in these ways: have long vowel sounds or don't have long vowel sounds; have one syllable (or beat) or have more than one syllable (or beat); have a blend (for instance, *snake, frog, worm*) or don't have a blend.

☐ **4.** Write *glide* and *hump* on a sheet of paper. Point out the word families *-ide* and *-ump*. Together, brainstorm, write, and read other words that rhyme and belong to the word families.

☐ **5.** Together, choose two or three words from the poem. Add them to your word wall and practice these words daily. Or add them to your child's word bank (a collection of words on cards, one word per card).

Maytime Magic

A little seed
For me to sow . . .

A little earth
To make it grow . . .
A little hole,
A little pat . . .
A little wish,
And that is that.

A little sun,
A little shower . . .
A little while,
And then, a flower!

—Mabel Watts

Maytime Magic

Looking at Words and Letters

☐ **1.** Ask your child to number all the lines that begin with *A*. Ask, *How many lines did you find?*

☐ **2.** Ask your child to find two lines that have four words and to circle each word in the two lines.

☐ **3.** Show your child the word *little*. Say, *Find and underline each* little.

☐ **4.** Say, *Point to the first line in the poem. Point to the last line in the poem. Point to the longest line in the poem. Point to the shortest line in the poem.*

Playing With Sounds

☐ **1.** Say, *Answer the riddles with words that rhyme with* wish. *I am a plate.* (dish) *I live in water.* (fish) *I go with splash.* (splish)

☐ **2.** Say, *Let's start with* shower. *What if we changed the first sound to "t"? to "p"? to "fl"?*

☐ **3.** Say, *Let's clap the beats while we read the middle stanza of the poem. How many syllables (or beats) are in each line?* (4)

Beginning to Read

☐ **1.** Say, *Write the word* seed. *Now change the first letter to make what we do for a baby at lunchtime.* (feed) *Now change the middle letters to make a word that means "things you can eat."* (food) *Now add a letter near the beginning to make what happens to a river after it rains a lot.* (flood) *Now change the last letters and add -er to make what a seed can become.* (flower)

☐ **2.** Ask your child to circle five words that have long vowel sounds. (*seed, sow, make, grow, hole, while*)

☐ **3.** Write *that* and *wish* on a sheet of paper. Point out the *-at* and *-ish* word families. Together, brainstorm, write, and read other words that rhyme and belong to the word families.

☐ **4.** Together, choose two or three words from the poem. Add them to your word wall and practice these words daily. Or add them to your child's word bank (a collection of words on index cards, one word per card).

☐ **5.** Write the word *flower.* Together, write other words that rhyme with *flower* and have the same spelling pattern. (*tower, power*)

My Neighborhood

People move in,
People move out,
Little children play and shout.
Old people, young people,
In-between,
Make a lively neighborhood scene.

—Betsy Franco

My Neighborhood

Looking at Words and Letters

- ☐ **1.** Ask, *How many words are in the first line of the poem? How many words are in the second line of the poem?*
- ☐ **2.** Say, *Look at the first and second lines of the poem again. Do you see two words that are the same? Draw a box around these words.* Repeat.
- ☐ **3.** Ask your child to find and circle one word that starts with uppercase *M* and two words that start with lowercase *m*.

Playing With Sounds

- ☐ **1.** Say, *I'll stretch these words. You tell me what the words are:*
  pee...p...ull (people)
  mm..ooo...ve (move)
  pp...l...ay (play)
  sh...ow...tt (shout)
- ☐ **2.** Say, *Now you stretch out these words:* old, young, make.
- ☐ **3.** Say, *Let's clap the syllables or beats while we read the poem.*
- ☐ **4.** Say, *I will say a word. You say its opposite:* in, little, old, play.

Beginning to Read

- ☐ **1.** Say, *I'll say a word from the poem. You tell me if the word has a long vowel sound. People* (yes), *little* (no), *play* (yes), *between* (yes), *lovely* (yes).
- ☐ **2.** Ask your child to illustrate the poem, write a sentence about it, and read it to you.
- ☐ **3.** Say, *I'll say a word from the poem. You tell me how many syllables (or beats) it has. People* (2), *move* (1), *children* (2), *young* (1), *neighborhood* (3), *scene* (1)
- ☐ **4.** Write *shout* and *make* on a sheet of paper. Point out the word families *-out* and *-ake*. Together, brainstorm, write, and read other words that rhyme and belong to the word families.
- ☐ **5.** Together, choose two or three words from the poem. Add them to your word wall and practice these words daily. Or add them to your child's word bank (a collection of words on cards, one word per card).

Wait for Me

Wait for me
And I'll be there
And we'll walk home together,
If it's raining puddle pails
Or if it's sunny weather.

Wait for me
And I'll be there
And we'll walk home together.
You wear red
And I'll wear blue
And we'll be friends forever.

—Sarah Wilson

Wait for Me

★60★

★ Looking at Words and Letters

- ☐ **1.** Ask, *How many words in the poem end in the letter* e?
- ☐ **2.** Show your child the word *and*. Say, *Find and circle all the* and's.
- ☐ **3.** Say, *Find two lines in the poem that start with* And. *Count and circle the words in each line.*

★ Playing With Sounds

- ☐ **1.** Say, *I'll stretch some words. You tell me what they are:*
  wh...aay...te (wait)
  wh...eee...ll (we'll)
  w...al...k (walk)
  wh...eth...er (weather)
- ☐ **2.** Say, *Clap your hands if these words start the same:*

  wait, weather **puddle, pails** **for, forever** **together, weather**
- ☐ **3.** Ask, *What word do you make when you take the last sound off the words* home, wait, pails?

★ Beginning to Read

- ☐ **1.** Ask, *What are the two most important words in the poem? Why do you think they're the most important?*
- ☐ **2.** Make word cards for *I'll, we'll, it's, I will, we will,* and *it is*. Play Concentration together. The object is to match the contraction with its longer form (for instance, *I'll* with *I will*).
- ☐ **3.** Say, *Circle all the words that have the long "a" sound. Be careful! Some are not spelled with just an* a. (wait, raining, pails, wear)
- ☐ **4.** Write *nail* and *and* on a sheet of paper. Point out the *-ail* and *-and* word families. Together, brainstorm, write, and read other words that rhyme and belong to the word families.
- ☐ **5.** Together, choose two or three words from the poem. Add them to your word wall and practice these words daily.

References & Resources for Further Learning

Dowhower, S. L. "Effects of repeated reading on second-grade transitional readers' fluency and comprehension." *Reading Research Quarterly*, 22 (1987): 389–407

——— "Repeated reading revisited: Research into practice." *Reading and Writing Quarterly*, 10 (1994): 343–358.

Herman, P. A. "The effect of repeated readings on reading rate, speech pauses, and word recognition accuracy." *Reading Research Quarterly*, 20 (1985): 553–564.

Kuhn, M. R., and Stahl, S. A. "Fluency: A review of developmental and remedial practices." (CIERA Rep. No. 2-008.) Ann Arbor, MI: Center for the Improvement of Early Reading Achievement, 2000.

National Reading Panel. "Report of the National Reading Panel: Teaching children to read. Report of the subgroups." Washington, DC: U.S. Department of Health and Human Services, National Institutes of Health, 2000.

Padak, N., and Rasinski, T. "Fast Start: A promising practice for family literacy programs." *Family Literacy Forum* (in press).

Padak, N., and Rasinski, T. "Fast Start: Successful literacy instruction that connects schools and homes." *College Reading Association Yearbook* (in press).

Pinnell, G. S., Pikulski, J. J., Wixson, K. K., Campbell, J. R., Gough, P. B., and Beatty, A. S. "Listening to children read aloud." Washington, DC: U.S. Department of Education, Office of Educational Research and Improvement, 1995.

Postlethwaite, T. N., and Ross, K. N. "Effective schools in reading: Implications for policy planners." The Hague: International Association for the Evaluation of Educational Achievement, 1992.

Rasinski, T. "Fast Start: A parental involvement reading program for primary grade children." In *Generations of Literacy—Seventeenth Yearbook of the College Reading Association*, edited by W. Linek and E. Sturtevant, 301–312. Harrisonburg, VA: College Reading Association, 1995.

Rasinski, T., and Hoffman, J. "Oral reading and the school literacy curriculum." *Reading Research Quarterly*, 38 (2003): 510–522.

Rasinski, T., and Padak, N. "How elementary children referred for compensatory reading instruction perform on school-based measures of word recognition, fluency, and comprehension." *Reading Psychology*, 19 (1998): 185–216.

Rasinski, T., and Stevenson, B. "The effects of Fast Start Reading: A fluency-based home involvement reading program, on the reading achievement of beginning readers." *Reading Psychology* (in press).

Samuels, S. J. "The method of repeated readings." *The Reading Teacher*, 32 (1979): 403–408.

Stevenson, B. "Efficacy of the Fast Start family tutoring program in the development of reading skills of first-grade children." Ph.D. diss., Ohio State University, 2002.

FAST START™

SCHOLASTIC

FAST START™
SCHOLASTIC
FAST START™
SCHOLASTIC
FAST START™
SCHOLASTIC
FAST START™
SCHOLASTIC
FAST START™
SCHOLASTIC
FAST START™
SCHOLASTIC
FAST START™
SCHOLASTIC
FAST START™
SCHOLASTIC
FAST START™
SCHOLASTIC
FAST START™
SCHOLASTIC
FAST START™
SCHOLASTIC
FAST START™
SCHOLASTIC
FAST START™
SCHOLASTIC
FAST START™
SCHOLASTIC

Scholastic Teaching Resources STK9625769 *Fast Start for Early Readers* PO# 80469

Scholastic Teaching Resources STK9625769 *Fast Start for Early Readers* PO# 80469